THE MONDAY MORNING CHECKLIST

A Guide for Leaders in a Busy World

Copyright@2019 by Jerry Philip Cooper

All Rights Reserved. Copyright under Berne Copyright Convention, Universal Copyright Convention, and Pan-American Copyright Convention. No part of this book may be reproduced, stored in a retrieval system, or transmitted in any form, or by any means, electronic, mechanical, photocopying, recording, or otherwise, without the express written consent of the author and/or the publisher (where applicable); except in the case of brief excerpts in critical reviews or articles.

Arrangements can be made for bulk purchases for sales promotions, corporate gifts, or educational purposes.

All inquiries shall be addressed to Jerry P. Cooper at 14730 Perthshire Road, Unit B, Houston, TX 77079. All electronic communication shall be through info@cdci-mediation.com

THE MONDAY MORNING CHECKLIST

A Guide for Leaders in a Busy World

Introduction

Leaders of companies and organizations of any complexity or size never have enough time. This book is not intended to throw a lot of analysis at you or burden you with any new theories. You know how to lead and that is why you are in the position you hold. So what will you find inside the covers of this book?

This book can be read as such or it can work as a desktop manual providing a framework or a set of guidelines for leaders who confront a demanding environment each and every day. Individuals who have responsibility over a significant number of people and resources do not need to be trained in how to be a leader. They do need to take advantage of any opportunity that helps them manage the scarcest resource of all – time.

This book is not aimed at those who wish to become leaders because it is not a leadership training book. It doesn't mean the book won't be helpful to those new to a managerial or supervisory position, but the thrust of this leadership guide is aimed at those who can most affect a company's revenues. Those not involved in the kind of leadership role discussed in these pages can still derive significant benefit from reading and using this book, and I encourage all who decide to use it to do so with diligence.

The central thrust of this book is to help capture that part of a leader's schedule where he or she can derive the most benefit when that leader is at the office. The title of this book recognizes a fundamental fact about leaders of large or complex organizations; they are always among the first to arrive at work.

They do not live their professional lives according to a defined amount of time at work. While many get up when it is still dark, go to work and go home after the sun has gone down, these leaders are where they are because they got up earlier and got home later.

In many organizations where the published work rules require employees to work from 8:00 AM to 5:00 PM, written or unwritten rules exist that executives are to be at work at least 30 minutes before everyone else. This rule is not generally discussed because in many organizations it is a "writ" that is inherent in that organization's culture.

However, as stated above, the leader is there at least one hour or more before the unofficial start time. This book, functioning as a guide, therefore, is based on the premise that this unique audience of one starts his or her day at 6:00 each morning.

This prototypical executive starts his/her day at this time of the day every day, and for the purposes of the subjects raised in these pages, it is being assumed that the leader's calendar is adjusted weekly to meet those demand known and understood before the work week starts and that he/she has the flexibility to respond to critical unknowns.

That said, I will the make note of the book's title and will further argue in the pages of this book that the prototypical leader's best chance to maximize his own efforts in carrying out his or her duties is to engage with these ideas on Monday morning.

Those who choose to use the framework that each chapter creates will find the book is not cluttered with a lot of graphs or visual aids.

A few aids will be used and I hope the reader will find them useful. This book covers nine (9) subjects. Once you begin, you may be tempted to tackle more than one subject in a particular week, but whenever you think about doubling up, I invite you to reconsider, and the reasons will become evident as you work through the different sections. The book will cover a period of eight weeks and always the first hour on Monday morning beginning at 6:00 AM.

So let's start by looking at that first hour and anchor the first premise. You do not focus on Monday's tasks – you know what those are before you walked in the door.

The probability is high that you called one or more of your executives on the way to the office, and they will be on top of what is immediate and necessary. Around 7:05 your executive assistant will open the door to the office with the calendar, the schedule, and the "list" of what is immediately in front of you for that day. You are ready for the day before you walked into your office.

Your task then is to use that first hour to focus on your leadership role. You are the strategic leader as well as the senior executive and it is the one obligation/responsibility that does not get the time it deserves. Strategic thinking is one of the key responsibilities of the leader and this fact is reflected in what the great thinkers and writers examine in their own writings.

I am not the first to suggest the importance of Monday morning. If you read Bernard T. Ferrari's book, <u>Power Listening; Mastering the Most Critical Business Skill of All</u>, you know that he concludes his book with a number of suggestions for leaders to think about as they start their week. His thinking and mine will no doubt overlap to some degree, but I feel confident that what is covered here adds to and/or complements what others write about, and yet offers a fresh perspective.

Successful leadership is based on an array of skills that need to be gathered, ordered, and blended into a seamless whole in order for the leader to be effective. For example, one of those skills, Vision, is such a key ingredient of that mix that no leader truly succeeds without it.

In John Maxwell's book, <u>The 21 Irrefutable Laws of Leadership</u>, he makes clear the relationship between vision (strategic thinking) and successfully navigating something to a successful conclusion.

In his Law of Navigation, it is the leader who sees the whole picture and can "see" the destination more clearly than anyone else—"before the ship leaves the dock."

The second premise is to understand the relationship between and among events.

What needs to be examined is, in many instances, the relationship between a leader's vision and the reality that is the responsibility of those who he/she has tasked with turning that vision into something real.

Jack Welsh stated in one of his most famous speeches that "The leader's unending responsibility must be to remove every detour, every barrier, to ensure that vision is first clear, and then real."

In the course of the nine weeks, as you think your way through this first hour of the week, one of the areas that you will want to look at will be the actions by your key executives to change or modify your vision as they seek to achieve immediate and near-term objectives. This is just one of the gaps between expectation and execution that you will focus on in the coming weeks.

So let's begin.

Chapter I

Work the Plan

Many of you reading the title of this chapter will be saying *what the heck*? "Work the Plan" sounds like I am stating the obvious. After all, how many times have you heard that exact phrase? Fifty, a hundred; probably, too many to count. One hears that phrase so many times it is easy to dismiss its relevance to the ultimate success of just about anything.

On television and in popular print, you often hear the protagonist (the main character) state dramatically that "the plan will last only until the first shot is fired." In the business world, there is fierce debate as to how effective business plans ultimately are. I stand in the camp that says "plans matter," especially if they accurately capture the leader's vision of what he or she wants to accomplish and the values the leader wants incorporated into the process.

Regardless of what popular literature suggests, for a leader to be successful a plan is indispensable. Ideas are elusive and not fully internalized until they are put down in writing, and a leader's team cannot successfully carry out the leader's vision until they can hold the written plan in their hands.

One example I use is the way General Eisenhower often operated when he was President of the United States. He took office shortly after the Korean Conflict ended, and his primary goals were twofold: avoid a war with the Soviets, which would have involved the use of nuclear weapons, and avoid a land war in Asia with China. He wrote this plan with the assistance of a few trusted advisors, and he adhered to it through most of his two terms in office.

Much of what was carried out would not be known for many decades, but what is notable is the length of time Eisenhower's team was able to carry out the elements of this plan largely as it was originally drafted.

History tells us that while President Eisenhower kept this overarching strategy a secret, he was known to demand detailed plans from each of his agency and department heads. He threw aside their attempts multiple times until he got what he believed was necessary for the effective operations of the government, which in that era was much smaller than it is today. Agency heads and department secretaries had a more hands-on approach, and he replaced several cabinet secretaries during his tenure who did not meet his expectations.

When Eisenhower adopted a plan, he demanded it be adhered to, because he believed it represented the best marriage of public policy and public dollars. He also gave the agency heads and cabinet Secretaries freedom to execute the details.

In this highly politicized world, historians often criticize the fact that Eisenhower played golf too often, but they miss the crucial point that he had tested the people running the departments under his administration. He knew their capabilities and he trusted them.

Many who read about him today view him through the lenses of popular literature and commentary, and may miss what set him apart from many of his peers in the military of that period. People forget that he studied engineering at West Point and was a superior student of mathematics.

It was his ability to both see the big picture and evaluate risks. Today we call that skill Quantitative Analysis. He used the skills he learned at West Point differently from what was the norm and was able to separate himself from the typical military officers of his day.

As he advance in his career, his ability to assess risk would prove critical to his future success as leader of the allied forces during World War II.

It boiled down to separating the difficult into manageable components – making the complex simpler; a task that still challenges leaders of today. He succeeded by developing/adopting a square matrix with four boxes inside the large box as illustrated by the figure below.

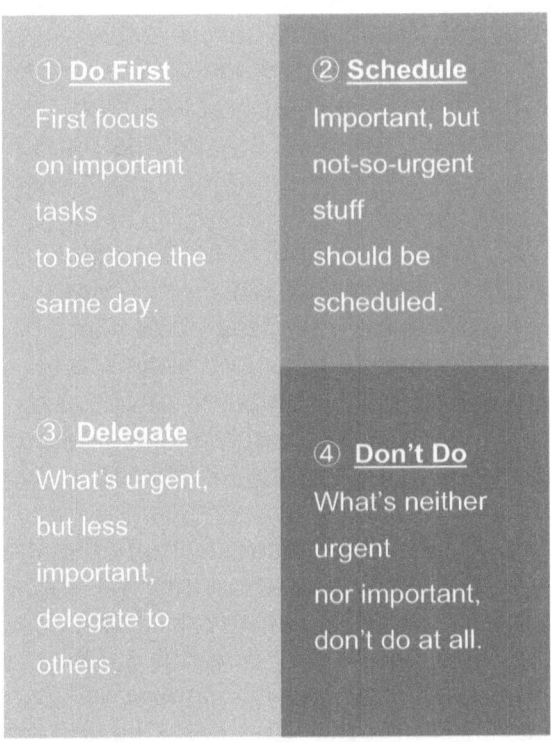

What we know of President Eisenhower is that he used this method of analysis consistently for more than 40 years. However many other tools and techniques he may have used, this was his "go to" methodology.

From our own experiences we know the four square grid is a very flexible way of looking at a range of issues. Whether you have studied Total Quality Management, Kepner-Tregoe, Myers-Briggs, or other similar managerial processes, many of us either used this process, or still do.

In modern organizations, the role of a leader is demanding in its scope and the foundation of this role is the leader's vision. Working the plan has a completely different look and feel to it at a leadership level. Anywhere else in the organization, what is seen, adopted, and acted on is a piece of something larger. It is the leader, and the members of his/her leadership team who see the whole of the plan. And because he knows the complete plan, he/she must have the ability to adapt as circumstances demand.

Every once in a while, a word or a phrase is used in popular literature and the use of that word or phrase spreads such that its relevance becomes diluted and almost meaningless. I frequently hear people in the business community talk about a particular leader and they offer the opinion that such and such a leader is so successful because he or she can "think outside the box."

I shake my head when I hear this because they miss the obvious that by saying that they are accusing that leader of being inside a box for most of what he/she does, and only stepping outside of it when he or she has to. Most of the leaders I know have a great deal of control over the environment in which they operate, and I always find that expression to miss the point by a wide margin.

In this chapter and in each of the other chapters as well, I will use an example drawn either from history or from the pages of current events to emphasize the subject matter discussed in each of the chapters.

This book is not an exercise in the case study method as the purpose of this book is not to engage the reader in a lengthy program of study, but to help people in leadership roles who read this book think about the specific subjects in these chapters as a way of clarifying their thinking.

Continuing with the example of President Eisenhower, many of us today see that period of time through the prism of history, and often have a distorted view of what he accomplished. Most people today do not know how unstable the Soviet Union was in the years immediately after Joseph Stalin's death, and most people of that era weren't aware either.

President Eisenhower and a few of his closest advisors knew the true situation. He was under enormous pressure to take this path or that path, and his critics were legion.

But he stayed true to his strategy and while the plan that supported his strategy did get adjusted as circumstances changed, the core strategy held up. By 1959, what he laid out with that first team of leaders got the job done, and he knew that any new administration would be on much more solid ground.

I encourage those readers undertaking this adventure to add Evan Thomas's book <u>Ike's Bluff: President Eisenhower's Secret Battle to Save the World</u>.

The following exercise will enable you to take that broad reach and narrow the focus during the first hour of each Monday morning.

12

This picture will appear in each section of this book. It represents visually that part of each hour this book discusses.

From your own perspective, it can be your grandfather's pocket watch that you keep in your coat pocket, the digital readout on your cell phone, or the clock on the wall near your desk. The graphic is divided into the classic four quadrants, each representing 15 minutes.

And here you are. You had a busy weekend that was relatively stress free. You were able to focus on family, perhaps play golf or tennis, and generally think about things other than work. Now the weekend is over, and you are at your desk.

1. Think about what happened.

In the first 15-minute segment, don't write anything down.

The purpose of this segment is to focus on what happened last week and *only* last week. I emphasize this because you'll want to avoid a cascading effect that can come into play; thinking about the previous week may lead you to think about something that happened the week before last. So the objective is to think solely about events that transpired last week.

There is also the temptation to insert thoughts about what is coming up today, and this too is to be resisted. Look only at the decisions you made last week, the actions you took, the things you handed off and to whom you handed them.

You are encouraged to think of this as reviewing a map of terrain you crossed. Think about the landscape you traveled over, and review in your mind the more obvious features, then narrow your focus to those features you remember but that initially did not stand out.

At this point you will begin to reorder things in your mind, saying to yourself, "that event was well executed, that one was a surprise because it came to us before we were ready," and so on.

As you think about and reorder them in your mind, look at four important events and pick two that you believe were *most* important. Again, you may be tempted to add to the number, but my recommendation is four.

Sometimes you will find that two events are interrelated and can be examined together. Your challenge, however, is to look at a balance of major and minor decisions.

2.   List the Events Chosen

Every day you make decisions across a wide range of issues, and you do this because you have an experienced team to back you up. You know your abilities and you know theirs, so you don't second guess yourself—at least not often. Your executive mind has valid reasons for prudently selecting the four issues or events you chose.

With the first 15 minutes of your Monday Checklist complete, write down the events you thought about most during that segment of time. Each decision will fall into one of several typical categories and these are only offered as examples.

a.   It involves a major capital expenditure that you and your team are watching closely.

b.   It involves an important client/customer.

c.   It involves ongoing regulatory obligations.

d.   It involves performance issues, either in terms of delivery of product or service or in the performance of an individual in a key role.

At the risk of stating the obvious, there is one key proviso. The decisions you are looking at do not represent a one-time action, such as "Please have John draft an answer to the letter from Congressman Blowhard." It involves assigning ownership and committing resources to an intent that will ultimately yield a discrete piece of work.

Begin your next 15-minute segment with the two minor issues that you selected. They are minor only in the sense that they are not major issues as you would typically define them.

Also write down the category each decision falls into, and examine it as part of this exercise. You picked these events/issues because you see this type fairly often and you have confidence in your ability to deal with them.

It's time to recognize a common truth: about 10% of the time something we normally treat as routine isn't routine at all. (This goes against the normal 80-20 rule, we subjectively use to assess consequences.) The problem here is that we often don't recognize the non-routine nature of an event until the adverse consequence hits.

Take the first of the minor issues you chose and think about where this type of issue falls in your plan. I encourage you to look at whether or not it is being handled in the right place by the right people. Again, you are not second-guessing yourself in the normal meaning of that phrase; you are testing whether or not your understanding of a certain type of issue still holds.

One of the key abilities of a leader is understanding that past decisions are a foundation for future success, just as past mistakes form the foundation for better performance in the future.
That sentence is worth repeating, so you might want to read it again. It is important to be aware of any shifts in your landscape. Sometimes, however, those shifts are not seen in time to avoid disruptions in the processes you have in place.

The probability is that the process still fits. You can then proceed to the next item and repeat the examination: who you assigned it to and how it fits into your current structures. Will the positive results of that event conform to the decision you made?

As you work your way through the next two items, stay within a 15-minute time block. Your objective is to recognize any variables you did not already consider. If an unforeseen variable exists, perhaps it is a low-probability risk. That's okay. An unforeseen variable does not necessarily change how you saw the issue when you made the decision.

When this phase of the exercise is completed, you will find that: a) all of your decisions stand, or b) a particular variable causes you to re-think all or part of one of the issues/events selected.

3,   Look out beyond this week and the next

The purpose of this block of time, again only 15 minutes, is to look at events that are planned four to six weeks out. This is not a Schedule Review Exercise, although you may notice some similarity in the terms.

We are operating on the premise that you have one or more major initiatives underway; also under the premise that each of these initiatives has a written plan prepared by one or more of your key staff.
The plans they have prepared are likely quite detailed and are accompanied by schedules with differing levels of detail to support the plans.

This is an event-oriented exercise. Any plans that exist are based on the strategy that you articulated, and you very likely have a high-level written strategy on which the plans were developed. In fact, the plans exist to support the strategy, to give it meaning and substance. The strategy has (or should have) key execution points.

Those execution points are what this exercise asks you to think about. In this block of time, review one of the major projects/initiatives and compare the plan and the strategy four to six weeks out. The purpose is not to test the plan, but to examine it for inconsistencies between your strategic overview and the current tactical decisions.

Take the four items you selected and examine them in relation to the strategy you developed. When you align these four items with their program phase against the strategy, do they line up programmatically with your vision of the desired end result?

I tell clients that this exercise will often validate that the programmatic phase reflected in the schedule will conform to the strategic thinking on which the plan was developed, but not always. Variations to the plan are often subtle events and not always identified in a timely manner. Yet, when you test assumptions against the strategic overview, inconsistencies and variations in the program phase can become clearer.

The purpose of this chapter and questions raised here is to make sure you are not neglecting the vision that will define the success you want the company to achieve. You and your team cannot effectively work the plan unless you periodically test past assumptions against a point in the intermediate future.

Do the assumptions and decisions still hold? Does your strategic vision as the "Navigator" stand true?

4. Ask the Right Questions

You ask questions every day. Much of what you process each day is based on the questions you ask. Your leadership team continually gives you information in response to the questions that flow continually across your desk. This last segment of the hour is about the questions you don't have time to ask, at least not often.

Chief executives and other senior leaders are highly confident individuals and are not in the habit of questioning their own decisions. Many view such an exercise as second guessing, which they see as a waste of time.

The right questions to ask now are not reflective questions. They clarify direction by connecting recent events to key actions in the intermediate future. Typical questions might be:

- What was it about these four (perhaps five) issues that grabbed my attention?
- Will they matter four weeks from now?

The first part of this exercise was to sift through the multitude of events/issues that crossed your desk the previous week and decide which are crying out for your attention. Any analysis of "why" was not the focus of that part of the exercise.

The key concept in this desktop manual is to focus your thinking in short periods of time and narrow your focus to what is essential.

You do not have a lot of time to generate four or five questions on which to build this part of the exercise. What kind of questions should you try to answer here?

Will a question that immediately comes to mind bring perspective to specifics of your company's goals, or does the question lead you to focus on your personal goals?

Considering personal goals is not a bad thing, as they can also benefit your company, but are you distinguishing between the two?

You should have one "why" question. Many who write about leadership offer conflicting points of view on the value of why questions. My view is that "why" questions are not constructive when something goes wrong and you are in the middle of the failure analysis. Later, after that analysis is done and corrective actions are in place, then the why question can be asked.

The question should focus on one thing - *why* the major cause went unnoticed. Allow me to reiterate: this exercise is not about failure analysis. Asking the why question at the right time brings the opportunity to reflect on what went wrong outside the crisis of the moment.

Accordingly, this reflection allows you as the leader to look at essential processes and systems and build changes where and if needed. If you use this approach consistently, you will find that the time you and your team take to think things through, along with holding the why questions for later, produces more positive and longer lasting results.

Chapter 2

On the Art of Listening

One of the most important skills, and a key ingredient that separates a leader from the rest of the crowd, is the ability to listen. Does this mean that you can't achieve a leadership role without this skill? No, it doesn't. A person can achieve leadership in a company or organization without good listening skills, but the chances of doing well in that position are significantly diminished.

I am periodically reminded of this in my own consulting experience, and this deficit is recognized by others as well. In a recent article in the Harvard Business Review on this subject, the author noted a survey that indicated as many as 25 percent of CEO's were not good listeners or were downright bad at it. The article went on to explain that poor listening skills at that level of leadership can have severe consequences to the point of damaging a company.

When such a gap exists at the top level, where information has already been funneled by the CEO's immediate reports, imagine what the absence of this skill would mean for the head of a major business unit who must communicate and receive feedback from other business unit leaders. Information flows up an organization, so cross-pollination among the various organizations is difficult.

It is made more difficult if the person in charge of the organizational structures does not listen well. The dominant theme in much of the relevant literature is that listening is an active skill as opposed to a passive attitude. Any leader worth his or her salt will tell you, "of course it is," but many people misunderstand what active listening actually means.

They have a perception that successful leaders have the ability to listen better than most and that the ability comes naturally. It may seem that way, yet the reality is that good listening skills are acquired through practice. Like competitive athletes who spend hours practicing, good leaders look for opportunities to refine their ability to actively listen.

If you focus entirely on active listening, however, you may fail to understand the foundation of this vital proficiency. Active listening is only a dimension of what is now called Empathic Listening. Today's successful leaders are learning early in their careers that listening is part of a communication process that works to reduce or eliminate misunderstandings.

Stephen R. Covey understood that listening, especially empathic listening, requires training. Some leaders trained themselves to achieve this level of listening, while other leaders found a qualified trainer to teach them the skill.

In chapter 5 of his book, *The Habits of Highly Effective People,* Stephen Covey wrote that there are several principles of communication. He begins by saying, "seek first to understand then to be understood."

When Covey wrote his book some 30 years ago, the idea that you first needed to understand the person you were talking to was a completely foreign concept to the vast majority of people. In the business world, the concept was seen as impractical.

That view was not hard to understand, in that most communication at the time was directive in nature: the boss told his employees what to do and when he wanted it done. The employee was then expected to figure it out.

Over the past 30 years, the notion of effective communication has undergone a revolutionary change. Good communicators, especially leaders, understand that skilled listening involves more than merely comprehending the words; it also involves understanding body language, emotion, and the way words are expressed (tone, volume, etc.). I believe Stephen Covey's book was one of the key drivers in this revolution.

This desktop manual would not be complete without asking the reader to examine his or her proficiency level in this important skill. As noted in the previous chapter, this workbook is based on a series of exercises that fit within a one-hour time frame. This chapter asks the reader to continue with this process.

1. What did you hear?

In Chapter 1, I asked that you look at actions and/or events that occurred in the prior week.

You are now in week two of this workbook, and the actions and events you examined are two weeks behind you. The events of two weeks ago are not the focus of this first hour on Monday morning.

During the first quarter hour of this week's exercise, you are asked to think about conversations you participated in the previous week. The focus is not on specific actions or events, but on discussions and conversations held with your leadership team.

You are asked to reflect on those conversations. Many of them likely involved normal give-and-take, wherein you and your team looked at issues, discussed options, outlined potential courses of action, and identified key activities. For the purposes of this exercise, I am making the assumption that you have the skill summarized briefly in the opening of this chapter. So the purpose of this hour is not to examine your active listening skills as such.

Instead, for the first fifteen minutes, think about what was discussed and ask yourself if there is something you may have missed. In a conversation or series of conversations on a complex issue, Peter Drucker observed that "the most important thing in communication is to hear what isn't being said." Whether it is a conversation or a negotiation, what is disclosed may not be, and often isn't, the whole story.

Choose three or four of the issues that required a serious conversation with one or more of your team. Think about those discussions and spend this time examining the picture of those issues that you hold in your mind.

2.   Check the Discipline

Now that you have thought about them, write them down. They do not have to be in any particular order.

Take this next block of time and look at how well you managed those discussions.

Listening, when done well, buys the leader time. The kind of listening being examined in this chapter involves discipline and control. In the next fifteen minutes, examine those conversations and, using the passage of time the weekend has given you, look back at those discussions and see if you maintained the discipline and control that allowed you to extract all of the salient information you needed.

Were the questions you asked focused on bringing order to information that initially never seemed to have any order? Did the questions prevent you and the others from recycling what had been discussed? Did your team get what they needed?

In his book, *Power Listening,* Bernard Ferrari provides a series of excellent examples of why listening is more than a skill but a discipline that must be practiced and controled. This is what I tell my clients, as well. What matters most to any leader is time, and when engaged in discussions, a leader cannot give up control of the conversation. It is his or her job to extract the information that matters and to provide the team with what they need to act on.

In this section, look at the questions above and apply them to the discussions of the previous week. Of the four issues you chose to examine in Chapter 1, did you maintain the control that you needed during the course of those discussions, and did you receive as complete a picture as possible in each of those issues? Is there a topic you want to examine further now that you are reflecting on the issues you chose?

3.   Engage in Deep Listening

The third quarter hour will pose a challenge. During this segment, you are asked to test the honesty inherent in how you listen to the person or group you are speaking with. A good coach tells his client that bad habits can creep into any process or routine, and an athlete or executive may not recognize the bad habit.

It is for this reason that you need someone you trust to use as a sounding board. Ask that trusted person to give you unfettered feedback about the way you listen to the subject matter that comes across your desk.

The term "Deep Listening" as I use it here is a relatively recent concept in communication. It was a concept used largely in the fields of music and meditation and now has come to have important relevance to the way successful leaders "seek first to understand, then to be understood."

Think of this process as slicing a ball in half, and looking at the layers exposed. The first layer is not very deep and represents the appearance of conversation rather than any substantial content. It's the pretense of listening until you can reasonably see him or her out the door.

The second layer is the type of communication that occurs in a casual conversation, whether at the end of the day, at a business meeting or conference or at a party. In this level, you are sustaining an existing business or professional relationship built on mutual respect and courtesy. The discussion topics are generally familiar to both parties and well understood by both.

The third layer is where empathic listening begins. This is the area where active listening takes place in its fullest form. It is where you construct a true understanding of who you are talking with and begin to understand the complete conversation.

Deep Listening is the last layer. At this level, you are listening to and understanding the total meaning of both the content and the emotion. In Deep Listening, you pick up the between-the-lines clues, understand what is not being said, and perceive hidden goals and objectives.

Look at your conversations from the previous week and examine each exchange carefully to determine if you applied the discipline of listening in a way that put you inside the empathic or the Deep Listening zone.

Pick one or two conversations to discuss with the person you use most often as a sounding board. The purpose is for him or her to hold up a mirror so that you can see if there are any faults or bad habits interfering with the overall effectiveness of your ability to listen deeply.

4.   Find the Questions

In this last segment, I want you to develop a series of questions that will aid you in thinking about improvements you can make in your ability to listen. In addition to discussing the subjects chosen in section three above, you will want to review these questions with that same trusted person.

The questions to ask yourself need to challenge you to be truthful about where you are as a listener and should also challenge you to be better. Essentially, the questions need to be about you. For example:

- How do others perceive me?

- Are there perceptions I am not aware of?

- Did I learn anything today?

In each section of this workbook, you will find a theme common to all sections. The last segment in each chapter is about looking at a picture four to six weeks ahead of you.

You want to examine what happened in the immediate past, and to think about it in the context of this one hour that is structured to direct your thinking in an ordered manner.

While there may be minor variations from chapter to chapter, the act of following a consistent structure allows you to stay in the present until you are asked to look forward. This last segment of each chapter is not about what happens on Monday or the rest of this week, but what is out there beyond this week.

CHAPTER 3

Adjust Your Priorities

Today's leaders understand that plans, goals and objectives will be impacted by change. This truth drives home a basic reality, and once you accept this basic truth, you can respond to changing conditions in ways that maximize your benefits and minimize the consequences.

Leaders of modern organizations understand this reality, which applies in all countries and almost every endeavor. Leaders who understand that change occurs rapidly and prepare for this reality succeed; those who don't fail. Those who understand the reality of rapid change build organizational structures with the capability of managing and resolving the changes that inevitably will occur and their attendant consequences.

An organization's ability to respond to change can have significant economic benefits, making those organizations more competitive. Therefore, it is no surprise that an entire industry developed and revolves around identifying change quickly and managing its effect on a company's or business unit's key objectives.

A range of tools, techniques, and computer software programs were created in response to this need. Companies with any degree of complexity have teams of people trained in the use of the tools and techniques.

I begin this chapter with this brief overview of change for the purpose of context. But it is not change that I want you to focus on in your role as a leader in this morning's exercise. I used the subject of change to set the stage for the true issue that lies beneath every change, and that is how to adjust priorities.

In a very real sense, adjusting priorities is an ever present responsibility. Whether as a CEO or the leader of a large agency, the ability to adjust priorities successfully is the hallmark of a good leader and often the making of a great leader.

I want to take a few minutes of your time to offer a couple of real-life examples to illustrate what I mean. In my work, and based on the dynamic of my relationship with each client, I will walk them through the story of Sir Ernest Shackleton's efforts to reach the South Pole.

Twice he tried to reach the South Pole first and failed, and when the Norwegian explorer Roald Amundsen got there first, Shackleton immediately began to plan a new expedition; one that was based on being the first to cross the Antarctic landmass. As the history books show, he failed in this effort as well.

Why is this story relevant to the leader of a modern corporation or organization? The answer is in the nearly 400 hundred days he and his team were marooned in an odyssey that lasted almost 500 days. From the books written about him, we know that he had a strong ego and was generally seen as a poor manager and decision maker.

An argument can be made that had he been a little more effective in his organizational skills, he might have achieved a different outcome.

Yet, in spite of his flaws, he was a charismatic leader with the ability to breathe life into his vision. He was able to earn the fierce loyalty of his men, which would be the foundation of his success in the 400 hundred days they were marooned.

Whatever flawed decision-making that resulted in their ship *The Endurance* being trapped deep in the frozen waters of the Weddell Sea, Shackleton understood that once the vessel could not escape, his priorities changed. It was no longer an expedition, it was a matter of survival.

He made it his goal to get everyone on that ship home alive. It is easy to visualize the hazardous open-boat voyage to Elephant Island, the decision to leave the bulk of his crew there, and the journey across more than 800 miles of open seas to a whaling station on a distant island to get help. This achievement within the overall odyssey is described in books and in movies.

What is harder to visualize, because it does not carry any high drama, are the ten months of living on a boat 144 feet long locked in the unyielding grip of winter's ice. Further, when the boat was eventually squeezed and broken apart by the massive pressure of moving ice, they survived for nearly six months living on the ice itself.

I encourage my clients to read about that expedition with a particular emphasis on those 16 months and to not focus so much on what came after, because that would not have been possible without understanding what Shackleton achieved during those 16 months.

At the heart of what he did was an intuitive understanding that he needed to master his priorities, adjust them, and change them into something his team could make their own, enabling them to survive one more day. His ability to create enthusiasm and motivate his men day in and day out was key to their ultimate survival, and the team's ability to adjust to the changes they faced almost daily is a testament to Shackleton's leadership skills, regardless of his other flaws.

I use the story of Sir Ernest Shackleton in my discussions with clients where I feel its message will be understood. The men and women who run modern organizations can too easily become insulated from the realities around them that, under the right circumstances, their failure to adjust the priorities of the company can cripple it; making it less competitive, making it a takeover target by a stronger competitor, and in rare cases cause it to fail. If Enron is not a strong enough example, then read about SwissAir.

The Switzerland airline's failure was not the most famous or the most spectacular, but it offers a textbook case on why failing to recognize changing conditions and failing to adjust priorities can lead to a disastrous outcome. As a case study, it offers several compelling examples on how changing conditions can overwhelm an organization when the leadership fails to react quickly enough, and how a bad situation can be compounded by too many actions taken with too little forethought.

Any of several blunders would serve as an object lesson, but one of the worst was the decision by the CEO and the Board of Directors of what was clearly a small regional airline to invest heavily in large long-distance aircraft, like the 747, the A310, and A321. Additionally, the CEO committed resources to this decision in an environment where merely maintaining their customer base would have been a major challenge.

With this background, the week's exercise will ask you to look at the priorities you examined last week. In each chapter, I will remind you in one form or another that this process is not asking you to second guess yourself but to look critically at how priorities are examined by you and key members of your leadership team.

1. Risk Assessment

During the first 15-minute segment you are asked to choose four key issues that had to be changed, moved, or adjusted from what was previously planned. Once they are written down, think about the role you played in the four examples and how you interacted with the other members of your leadership team.

The intent here is to examine in as detached a manner as possible how effectively your risk management processes were applied to the adjustment of priorities.

When surrounded by business vocabulary and concepts wrapped in vernacular, it is easy to overlook the basic purpose behind any risk assessment, which is to help and not harm the organization.

Adjusting priorities is a necessary prerequisite to implementing change. A leader's goal must be to assure that those changes have positive consequences and no unmanageable negative ones.

The four issues/priorities in this first segment should be examined with two questions in mind. First, in retrospect, were any of the adjusted priorities you examined last week low priorities? I generally pose this question first because there is a real tendency for leaders to focus on the easy priorities first.

Many CEOs avoid this trap, but a surprising number get snared in the low-priority trap. I describe it as a trap for the simple reason that when you allow yourself to be caught up in small tasks, they tend to multiply like field mice, consuming more and more of your time. In reviewing the issues from the prior week, did you avoid "playing in the minors?"

It is my hope that those of you who adopt this book and use it on a regular basis will always ask the second question at this point in the exercise. When it comes to adjusting priorities, you are affecting the outcome of the organization's goals and objectives, and potentially the future of your employees.

The second question asked here should almost always be: Are you being honest in the answers you give?

The tougher the question, the more honest you must be in your leadership role. The one unchangeable reality of any organization is that it operates on a defined and limited set of resources within the boundaries of the budget. When priorities must be adjusted, someone's ox is going to get gored. Programs and budgets may be changed, jobs may be affected and your leadership team must be as candid as conditions permit.

Personnel up and down the chain of command have to be in a position to make informed decisions; whether it's moving their piece of the work in a different direction, or whether it's an action affecting their careers.

If you don't have the answers, say so. If you can't provide the answers at that moment because you are not allowed to, say so. Withholding the truth or censoring it will sow the seeds of failure.

2. Resistance to Change

Leaders need to recognize and respect that adjusting priorities cannot be truly effective without taking into account the factors that create resistance to change. In the second segment of time, recognize that the four items/issues which you selected for review contained varying degrees of resistance or the potential for resistance. Your role as the leader of the organization will require you to consider a number of questions about the priorities you chose.

Among these potential questions are:

What assumptions, if any, did these adjustments challenge? Which recommendations did you initially agree with, and with which did you disagree?

As you work through these priorities that were adjusted, take a few moments to think about the ownership, responsibility, and everyone's favorite buzzword – accountability. Are the procedures/processes you have in place working for these three areas?

These are particularly important questions at this phase of the exercise. If not thought through carefully, the review and response to changes regarding which priorities must be adjusted can result in mixed messages about what is needed.

Your own experience teaches you that organizations often send out different, possibly opposing, messages and when different messages go out at the same time, the confusion can bring things to an abrupt halt. If your organization is of a certain size and scope, you likely have a company newsletter, and corporate videos are produced to convey important information.

When important changes need "selling" to the troops, key members of your leadership team are chosen to deliver the message. Subsets of the message are delivered through off-the-record discussions by managers and supervisors briefed on what to say.

The time frame immediately surrounding the adjusting of priorities and the processes designed for change management will likely provide opportunities for mixed messages to get out and proliferate through the rumor mill.

Looking at the issues selected, did you communicate the importance of being clear up and down the organizational structure? Did you communicate the importance of candor where possible, and clarity about what is known and what is not?

3. Recognizing the Reality

You have about half an hour before your executive assistant opens the door to your office. With him or her the tide will flow in, bringing with it both order and disorder. You know this and you are ready for what the day will bring. For this half hour, you will need to resist looking at the time you have left and continue to separate yourself from what is ahead today.

The first two segments ask you to isolate and identify issues, and then to think about those issues in the context of questions, both specifically and organizationally.

The remaining two segments ask you to look forward to a point beyond today or tomorrow. Each chapter asks you to pick a time frame six to eight weeks out to visualize as many potential consequences as you can, looking for both strengths and weaknesses.

You are viewing the organizational landscape six to eight weeks out. Some of the changing priorities you have set in motion are intended to modify that future landscape. You and the leadership team have a clear idea of what needs to be done. The desired end result eight weeks out (or within a time frame specific to your company), requires that you work back from that point in time visualizing how the changes need to be implemented.

This focus on working backwards is based on what you already know about change. The parts of the organization most affected by changing priorities do not absorb changes immediately. There is a time lapse such that performance is not reflective of the change. Brian Tracy speaks about this in his consulting work by reminding leaders that "the relationship between change and performance is not instantaneous."

The goal of this forward-looking exercise is not to "see" the desired end result working. The goal is to visualize how it is affecting work that needs to be changed in a way that helps you perceive where inefficiencies will mostly be felt. When you can anticipate where the learning curve will have the strongest impact, you can think about ways to mitigate that impact instead of assuming that is someone else's job.

What kind of questions should you be posing to yourself and your leadership team so that you and they can shepherd the changing priorities to the desired conclusion with best possible impact on employee performance?

As an example, will the implementing team or teams receive coaching on how to adapt to the changed priorities? Are there process-driven behaviors that need changing, and will the employees be trained on the behaviors at the correct point in the implementation process?

Each organization is unique, and there are questions in this segment that must be formulated and tailored to the specific organization. The key here is to generate a list of questions for you and your team to review, questions that test your assumptions about what the changed organization or work will look like eight weeks out; recognizing that eight weeks is illustrative only and the appropriate time frame is your decision.

4. Connecting the Links

One of the purposes of this workbook is to help you focus periodically on your vision in an ordered/structured manner. The linkage between The Plan(s) and the overarching strategy is important at any point. Yet, it takes on greater importance when the organization's operating objectives, experience changes that require you and your leadership to adjust the organization's priorities.

The process of responding to change can have a negative impact on the connections between the strategic vision and the subsequent plan. As the leader you will need to assure that linkage between the vision and the plan, even after it's changed, still holds.

Many CEOs and leaders of large organizations hold the belief that their vision is shared by all employees in the company. Sometimes that belief is justified; sometimes it's not. You do not want to be one of those leaders who is surprised to find that not everyone in your company shares your vision. You do not want to be in the 25 percent we talked about in chapter two.

The strategic vision belongs first to the organization's leader, because he or she is the architect of all of its parts and pieces and is the one who can see the totality of it better than anyone else. It also belongs to everyone else. The leader must pass it down to everyone in the organization and see that it is shared to the point that every individual in the organization becomes a stakeholder of that vision.

It is the employee -- not the leader -- who brings the vision to life. I have heard others say that the engine that powers the leader's vision is the employee's willingness to commit to that vision and make it his or her own. It is at the employee-engagement level where impacts on the organization will occur.

What are the questions you must take with you and seek answers to as part of this exercise? Each organization embodies a unique environment, and many of these questions must reflect that environment. But there are some important common themes such as:

- Who can best identify and assist you in minimizing distractions that would interfere with the changes in priorities?

- How can time best be used to advance the changing priorities and minimize their impact on the learning curve?

- What fits into the 80/20 rule and what does not?

And remember: trust your key leadership people.

Chapter 4

Take Action

Established leadership consultants and trainers such as John Maxwell, Seth Godin, Stephen Covey, and others of similar caliber speak and write about the importance of taking action. When you examine their advice, they are reminding us that in business nothing is static. In this chapter, I will be asking you to examine what you do to translate into actions the many ideas, problems and opportunities you confront.

When you pause for a few minutes, as I ask you to do in this weekly exercise, you are taking a snapshot of things that occurred in the recent past. This snapshot is a way of setting the stage for thinking about whatever is critical to your success as a leader. It is easy to fall into the mindset that what you are looking at is a static process which only moves when you act on it, and that is not the case. Before proceeding with the purpose of this chapter I want to put this subject in context.

I will start with an analogy I used with a recent client. He was having difficulty dealing with the gap between implementation and performance, and with how his people were responding in that lag time. As noted in the previous chapter, the lag time between implementation and performance is inevitable. To get past his frustration, I used the example of the electric dynamo.

Most people with basic knowledge of electricity understand that our modern electrical industry and most electrically powered devices, regardless of size, are powered using alternating current. That technology became the foundation of electricity as we know it, because it is more efficient than direct current. More efficient means less costly.

Dynamos on the other hand, produce direct current through the use of a device called a commutator. In the discussion with this client, I explained that one of the reasons the A/C motor won out over the dynamo was that it did not need the commutator. These devices (commutators) are less efficient because they are mechanical devices that need maintenance and repairs more frequently than other electromechanical devices.

I explained that he was like a dynamo generating direct current. The organization as a whole was his commutator. He was not recognizing that the inefficiencies of his "commutator" were outside his control. He was not understanding that his role was to recognize inefficiencies and design actions to minimize and/or mitigate that reality – that "given." In the same way that mechanical devices have limitations so do organizations. While he could accept that fact in the academic sense, he was having difficulty with the reality of it.

Even with one's best efforts, actions taken by leaders in response to changing priorities don't always have the anticipated outcomes. A good example of this is how J.C. Penny brought itself back from the brink of extinction. The story is by no means finished, but comparing where it is today with where the company found itself at the beginning of 2012 is worth a brief examination.

In the first quarter of 2012, in response to a second year of losses in excess of $150 million dollars, J.C. Penny suspended its dividend payment and identified more than 40 stores that would be targeted for closure. In 2010, the company put in place a long-term plan intended to reshape and transform how J.C. Penny delivered its products to consumers. In 2011, it stopped publishing its iconic catalogue, one of the most enduring symbols of its long history.

The company's management determined that everything had to be rebranded and anything that did not support the new vision for the company had to change.

In late 2010, as part of the long-range plan, a new CEO was brought in to lead the company in its new direction. He lasted just over 1.5 years and was replaced by his predecessor in April of 2013. In the spring of 2012, the new strategy was roughly two years old, and in a very real sense, its struggles were just beginning. The new CEO, Ron Johnson, moved too aggressively and tried to implement too many changes in too short of time – does this sound familiar?

By the end of the first quarter of 2013, sales had collapsed. By the summer of 2013, the company's debt had ballooned to more than four billion and, for the first time in its history, people were asking if J.C. Penny could avoid bankruptcy. As a consequence of these major missteps, the company's book value declined by more than 50% and it was forced to shed 19,000 jobs. The story is too long to cover here in the kind of detail that it deserves, but the fault for all these disastrous decisions goes all the way up to the board of directors. Governance during this crucial period was almost non-existent.

Enough people believed in the core elements of the strategic plan and continued to work the plan, that the blood bath of 2013 ended and the changes, battered and bruised though they were, finally began to show results. 2015 was seen as a success because revenues increased significantly, and solid growth was forecast for 2016. While profits remain in negative territory, jcpenny sees itself as beginning to finally turn it around. It is now re-growing its customer base, expanding sales, and will continue to aggressively manage costs to achieve profitability by the end of 2017.

Yet, this is just the end of the first steps in this company's transformation. J.C. Penney, under its new logo jcpenney, is getting ready to begin implementation of a new strategic vision, one that will help the company survive in the new world, where they must compete with Amazon and other online retailers.

The company still has many risks in front of it, but it seems to be one of the few retailers that has found a way to navigate out of the "retail ice age" that all retailers find themselves in.

It is a case study worth reading in that it offers telling examples of what can go wrong if you go too fast and important lessons on why leadership, courage, and patience are necessary for the long haul.

1. From Strategy to Action

The title of this first segment was chosen deliberately. Leaders of companies and organizations large or small are looking for the secret formula for success. The phrase "from strategy to success" can be found in the writings of college professors, business leaders, gurus and what have you. When you saw the heading, you probably winced. That is exactly the reaction I am aiming for.

Whether you are looking at a complex turnaround such as the one being experienced by jcpenney or you are reorganizing a critical project with the potential to significantly impact your bottom line, there is a strong commonality to the steps that leaders go through, the steps they think about taking, and most of all the urge to act.

Some companies are slow to wake up to the need to adjust their priorities, change their missions, and abandon what no longer works. When they do wake up, some of them hesitate and delay. But far too many tend to act too quickly.

This part of the exercise is asking you to look at the mission of the company or organization and the strategy(s) in place to deliver on that mission. Not revisiting that relationship is not only a serious mistake, but a mistake leaders often make. When this connection is examined in the context of major adjustments or changes, the leader can recognize disconnects and gaps in how the company's governance and other senior leaders understand of the link between mission and strategy.

When this connection is recognized, it is a short step to understanding and identifying a range of weaknesses that may have leaked into the organizational structure.

Those weaknesses may be creating areas of stress that aren't recognizable until the changes are examined in the context of the mission and the strategy.

For experienced leaders, managing change is not a new experience, and some leaders are also accustomed to looking for weaknesses, but many do not give this step enough effort and time. An experienced leader is familiar with the common push-back by others on his team of "we don't have time for that" or "the client will never go for it." The leader that is persuaded by these arguments sometimes learns an important lesson.

Begin by looking at the major decisions from the past week, and if one or two carried over from the prior week that is fine. Did any of these decisions involve a significant adjustment in priorities and change? Spend this time thinking about them, write them down, read them over and assess their significance. If you decide one should fall out of your initial assessment, go back and re-examine the list and add one back in; otherwise, we move to part two of this chapter.

2. The Weakness uncovered

This second segment asks you to look at what you wrote down and to check for weakness in the initial examination of the issues chosen and acted upon.

This segment comes close to asking you to second guess yourself. I have gotten push-back on this discussion in the past, but when handled correctly, this exercise sets up a critical examination of decision based on a process of deconstructing the decision to look at its component parts. Call it, if you will, a form of reverse engineering for which the purpose is to discover a hidden weakness.

Having read this, many leaders immediately will think: strengths, weaknesses, opportunities, and threats -- in other words a SWOT analysis. A leader of a large company or complex organization probably has numerous SWOT analyses available, and these may be available for one or more of the decisions recently acted on.

Since time is of the essence in this weekly one-hour process, the purpose here is to use your experience and unique position as the leader to see what others cannot see because they are not as close to the totality of the strategy as you are.

For example, in the issues you chose, is there the potential that one or more key people are holding back negative feedback or "bad news?" The processes governing change both large and small are almost always formalized. Has the level of detail and oversight of the change-management process become too formalized? Are these processes and procedures getting in the way?

The search for potential weakness must be examined from a point of view that is as free as possible of any assumptions. In the examples chosen, where the changes in priorities appear to be well received and accepted, the focus should be on *how* it was received.

There is a difference between compliance with a change in direction and support for the change. It is sometimes easy to mistake compliance for support, and where individuals fall in this distinction can be a source of future trouble.

It would not surprise me that the issues you are examining generated resistance from one or more of your key leadership team.

Your team is heavily invested in making their respective parts of the organization successful, and how they perceive the impact of the changes is often not a major point of discussion. How was the pushback resolved; or was it simply pushed below the surface?

3. A leap forward

This third segment is designed to focus on the period beyond the immediate. In this case, looking out six to eight weeks ahead may not tell you anything about impacts to the plan as it is presently configured. As noted earlier, adjusting priorities in a significant way takes time. The time from implementation to performance may well extend beyond the time frame used for the first three chapters. So how can this segment be utilized effectively?

I explained earlier that there is a bias on the part of line managers to act sooner rather than later, as they are focused almost exclusively on performance. They want any changes to be absorbed as quickly as possible so they can move on. Actions taken quickly will impact the alignment that links the strategy to the plan.

Change impacts existing alignment processes, and the areas where this initial misalignment can occur is what you as a leader must try to identify. Processes link functions and functions link products, and these core processes are what the customer sees. Not only do the key processes link the elements that make up the operations of a company, they are also linked to the company's strategy, and identifying where the processes align with the strategy is a key for the forward analysis in this segment.

So, what are the questions you should ask yourself? Are you comfortable with the performance indicators chosen to track the changes and/or new priorities?

I read an article not long ago where the writer used the analogy "line of sight" to illustrate his point about the relationship between the strategy, the key processes in place, and the plan. I found it an effective way of underscoring the relationship between changes to processes and ownership of those processes.

As a leader you should be looking at questions that drive you to examine who owns what piece of a given process and the changes affecting that ownership. One query that should be part of this segment is the "what's in it for them" question. How were the risk and reward questions addressed? Do the incentives carry the risk of perverse outcomes?

4. It Takes a Sale

This segment ends what I began in chapter three, where we talked about the importance of recognizing the need to adjust priorities and how to manage the impact of such adjustments on an organization. I also touched on the need to sell the new direction. We now return to that theme because it doesn't happen just at the front end.

This is something many experienced leaders know, but the day-to-day pressures a company's leadership faces often results in the sales job being ignored beyond an initial effort, or it is delegated to someone else. Selling the need for change and the adjustment of priorities that accompanies change can meet with the same difficulties that apply the in the story of a man leading a man blind from birth up to an elephant and by touch trying to explain to the blind man what the elephant looks like.

To the blind man, the explanation of the component parts will never make sense because he does not know what an elephant's trunk looks like. In modern organizations, the challenge is to keep the changes from becoming the elephant and to ensure that those who must own the changes are able to understand the whole picture.

The CEO and his/her leadership team own the change process from the changes to the mission, the strategy, the plan all the way down to its component parts. In order for significant change to take place, they have to sell the changes up and down the organizational structure.

This is a task that cannot be delegated to the line managers. Pieces of it, yes; after the rollout and a detailed orientation, component parts can be adopted by managers and supervisors, but the sale of the whole has to come from the leadership.

This last quarter hour is about the questions you want to discuss with your leadership team. In several chapters, this final section encourages you to develop a series of questions that you review with either a mentor or the person in the organization you trust most. In this chapter, you are asked to think about the questions that were flying back and forth last week and, based on your conclusions, find new questions to test yourself and your leadership team.

Are the issues clear? How are the changing priorities being constructed from a narrative standpoint? Does that narrative recognize the people issues that will be impacted? Is the morale of the employees a factor in the story that the leadership must sell?

Chapter 5

Problems are Always There

Several years ago I read an article in Forbes Magazine in which the author quoted Karl Popper, a 20th century philosopher of science, who said: "All life is problem-solving." This quote made me curious to know more, and this ultimately led me to my favorite quote by Karl Popper in which he said, "the best thing that can happen to a human being is to find a problem, to fall in love with that problem, and to live trying to solve that problem, unless another problem even more lovable appears."

I think the reason I like this quote is probably the same reason many business leaders would like it once they read it. A true leader wants to solve problems, and wants them to be interesting and weighty. For a leader, problems represent opportunities to make things work better, to create new products, processes and potential to expand into new markets.

This chapter will explore the fundamental fact about problems. They are the primary reason the leader is in his/her role. The thing that distinguishes a leader from an average run-of-the-mill executive is the ability to deal with problems. Leaders "see" problems differently. I will start with the simple fact that when confronted by a problem they do not waste time on the obvious; they quickly move beyond it.

They not only see the totality of it but also can see boundaries, while others have to spend time understanding the obvious before discovering these boundaries. This heightened skill of observation sets astute leaders apart like the master diamond cutter is separated from the average diamond cutter. A leader sees fault lines others do not. And they have patience.

The more experienced the problem solver, the more patience he or she can draw on. One more note from the 20th century. A word was often used in the middle of the last century that has since fallen from general use. I make reference to this word with some of my clients, and that word is linchpin.

A linchpin serves to hold together parts or elements that exist or function as a unit, and that analogy often defines what a leader does; especially when it comes to problem-solving.

As noted in an earlier chapter in this book; it is not about leadership per se. Leadership is one of the most closely studied aspects of human interaction. It would be an understatement to say that scholars across many disciplines have studied and written extensively about what makes a good leader and the skills someone needs to be successful in such a role. For me to add one more bucket of salt water into the ocean is a waste of your time and mine.

From one chapter to the next my goal is to help you focus for a specific amount of time each week on one aspect of that which makes you a success; a sifting through your skill set to examine if you are getting the most from a particular ability.

The purpose of this venture is to help you look at what you use on a daily basis to see if you can strengthen, add to, or expand the skill set that got you to where you are now.

All organizations have this one reality in common: the effectiveness and quality of problem-solving is a direct reflection of the leader's attitude. When he or she reflects a positive attitude toward problem-solving, it sends a clear message that problem-solving is worth the effort and time of his/her leadership team, and that attitude cascades through the organization.

Managers, supervisors, and employees see the expectation being created from the top down and respond accordingly.

The leader's attitude toward problem-solving quickly grafts itself to the organization's culture and can have a long-lasting effect on the culture as a whole. Problems cross the leader's desk every day, and solving these problems is a critical component of his/her role in the organization. The leader must possess a positive attitude to maintain momentum.

There is a compelling paradox in that one of a leader's most important tasks is to take the lead in solving problems, and one of his/her most important tasks is to minimize the occurrence of problems by anticipating them.

Before asking you to enter into the exercise portion of the chapter, I like to set the stage by using actual events, a brief case study so to speak, to put things in context. In this chapter, I will begin with an excerpt from the story of a company that made decisions which looked promising in the short term but did not end well.

The previous chapter focused on taking action in a macro sense. Here I will use an example to discuss the direct consequence of the problem-solving process – making decisions.

Any discussion about making decisions can be seen as a corollary to taking action as discussed in chapter 4 or viewed as re-stating the idea behind taking action. If you take the time to review the things that jcpenny has undertaken over a nearly seven-year span, you will quickly realize that the necessary decisions, both major and minor, number in the thousands.

My objective in this chapter is to look at decision-making as the immediate byproduct of the problem-solving process and how the decisions made can result in additional problems. Many of the sub-tier problems result from failure to anticipate future consequences, especially the farther out you go from the initial set of decisions.

Many companies have well developed risk analysis tools, techniques, and processes designed to map out multiple consequences stemming from any set of decisions. However, it is also a fact that these measures are all based on rules of statistical probability, and there is always a margin of error.

The further away you go on the decision tree, the less reliable future decisions become. Good leaders know this and make the effort to periodically check that actions/decisions remain in alignment with plans and strategy(s).

Yet the existence of these tools cannot eliminate but can only mitigate the failure to anticipate what failure analysis will later disclose that you should have known. Companies that use risk analysis tools and techniques effectively have the advantage of minimizing adverse consequences while advancing their strategic vision. But regardless of their competence and skill, even these companies eventually experience a change or event that was not anticipated.

How a company reacts, responds, and moves through this event will be unique to that company, and whether it is stronger or weaker because of the experience will stand as a testament to the skill and vision of the leader and his/her team. The example in this chapter illustrates this point.

At the risk of being repetitive, the use of examples in this book are intended to be brief explorations that illustrate the subject being discussed. I encourage readers to study these companies in more detail as time permits. Let's look briefly at Tesco PLC and its expansion outside of Great Britain. Our focus will be the decision of Tesco to enter the Korean market, how that was accomplished, and the result of that endeavor.

Tesco was founded just after WWI by a Royal Airforce veteran named Jack Cohen. With his separation pay, Cohen set up a roadside stand and sold groceries. From that modest beginning Tesco gradually expanded into one of the largest supermarket chains in Britain. In the 1970's and 1980's, it expanded to provide gasoline and a range of home goods in addition to its core supermarket business.

By 1990 Tesco needed to look outside of Britain in order to grow, and with the fall of the Soviet Union the company's management saw opportunities to enter new markets quickly. Between 1990 and 1997 Tesco opened stores in Hungary, the Czech and Slovak Republics, and Poland. Additionally, it expanded into India and Thailand. It was Tesco's initial success in Thailand that led to the decision to attempt an expansion into other Asian markets, and to its decision to focus on Korea as its next goal.

This case, like the others I introduced in earlier chapters, is too lengthy to discuss in detail, and I encourage you to read about it in depth to appreciate what worked well and what didn't. The case is a good example of a company that became the victim of its own success. I could easily take up the whole chapter on the dangerous mix that is created when hubris, ego, and quick success are mixed together.

Any review of problem-solving is incomplete without addressing its primary product – decisions.

Decision-making is what follows naturally from the problem-solving process, and it is that relationship between problem-solving and decision-making that I want to discuss. Tesco offers a practical real life example of what this interconnection looks like when it works and when it doesn't.

Experienced leaders know that decision-making is where the "die is cast" and where a whole host of things take place in an effort to ensure a successful outcome. When it works, a company makes money and gets to stay in the game. When it works really well, you get to grow. It can be particularly galling for a leader when success suddenly stops being a success and becomes a costly and painful failure.

In the 1990's, Tesco made a remarkably successful expansion into other markets by making successful acquisitions. In Eastern Europe, it expanded into home goods by buying K-mart stores that Sears did not want in its purchase of K-mart. It also bought companies in the home goods and grocery business.

Without much pause, it immediately looked to Asia and, in 1997, began negotiating with the Lotus Supercenter chain, which resulted in Tesco buying a portion of Lotus in 1998. While completing this deal, the company was also looking at Korea. In retrospect, it is curious why Tesco chose Korea for its second Asian expansion, because Korea was and is an extremely difficult market for foreign companies to operate in successfully.

Tesco had some appreciation of this. As with its decision to join an existing company in Thailand, it chose to partner with Samsung in Korea as a means of neutralizing the difficulties of being an outsider trying to do business in a country where business is all about relationships and close ties with the government.

The merger of Samsung and Tesco was launched in 1999 under the name Homeplus. The next 10 years appeared to affirm Tesco's strategy for its Asian markets. Homeplus quickly attracted the loyalty of millions of Koreans to ultimately number among the top five retailers in Korea. It appeared that Tesco had indeed found a successful formula for operating in the Asian market – until 2010. The recession of 2009, commonly referred to as the Great Recession, did not take long to make itself felt.

The recession exposed a major weakness in this partnership. There was no plan B and no strategy for reacting to dramatic changes. The next few years proved to be painful. A series of agonizing doses of reality resulted from the singular failure to understand that, in Asia, when things go south you had better have a good strategy for weathering the storm. Tesco/Samsung did not have the foresight to build an exit ramp or a way around the storm.

After riding the crest of the wave for 10 years and then being bounced around in the shoals for four years, Tesco exited the Korean market in 2015 after losing nearly two billion dollars over that four-year period. The sale put an end to what had initially appeared to be a model for long term success.

1. Making the leap

Before the advent of satellites and GPS systems, mariners and aviators mastered the science of navigation in order to locate and maneuver between a current location and their ultimate destination. Like a skillful mariner, astute leaders learn to quickly connect the dots and map out a realistic plan of action to achieve their objectives even in a storm.

The foundation of success lies in its ability to make the leap between problem-solving and decision-making in a manner that maximizes success and minimizes failure. Successful transition is achieved by seeing the barriers and preventing them from impeding the necessary actions the leader must take to achieve success.

Leaders look to a whole host of tools and techniques to aid in identifying ~~these~~ potential bottlenecks and roadblocks. I do not dismiss the range of tools and techniques that exist in the workplace; they are important resources in a leader's arsenal. But I offer an important caution. By moving too quickly in the direction of identifying which resources were needed, and when they were needed, more than a few leaders have created obstacles where none existed.

In this first segment of the weekly exercise, the issue is not in the use of Pareto Principles, critical path schedules or any of the processes now available, but in identifying when and where to add them to the decision-making process.

As in previous chapters, you are asked to look at key decisions that you had to make last week. What were the first steps you deemed necessary to reinforce the decisions that needed to be made? Before the decisions were made, what did you examine first? At the risk of overusing the mariner analogy, how do you employ the "map" on which you based the decisions you made?

Now that a period of days has passed, and as you examine last week's decisions, look forward across that six-to-eight-week time span. Did the factors you reviewed at the time anticipate the potential roadblocks?

2.   Break Down Silos

Earlier, I alluded to the challenges of communicating across organizational lines, and from my perspective, this is one of the well-known obstacles that never receives enough time and attention. That attention deficit is where I want to focus this part of the exercise.

Effective decision-making requires that communication be transparent across all functions. That may sound fairly straight forward, but inside organizational structures information naturally flows upward. In business and industry, the common term for this is the silo effect. Different organizations in a company may communicate with one another, but more often than not it is a controlled process that limits what information is disseminated.

Important and transformative decision-making does not roll through organizations freely. Information about important decisions often loses momentum and, because of the silo effect, the impacts of decisions are diminished.

In the second part of this week's segment, I want you to examine how you addressed the potential impact of the silo effect. Did you anticipate this potential impact?

While I am a fan of matrix-type organizations, they do not solve the silo effect. It may not be as severe, but the silo effect remains a real problem even in matrix organizations. In your organizational structure, what do you have in place to mitigate or prevent the silo effect problem?

People who are unsure of themselves have a natural tendency to push problems and decision-making up the chain of command regardless of the organizational structure. A leader who tackles this problem can be forgiven if he/she thinks it's solved.

To break through the silo effect and put a perceived solution in place requires a lot of effort, and the solutions often prove to be temporary.

3. People are the Key

The focus of the third segment in this chapter is the people you have in place to prevent normal day-to-day activities from impacting or distorting the decision-making that must flow freely through an organization.

It is critical that important decisions having significant impact be championed and defended by key people across the organizational boundaries, and these key people must have the necessary authority to be effective champions. When you look out six weeks and longer on the timeline, are key people strategically placed to connect the diverse interests?

In this Monday morning routine, are the answers to these questions generally positive? The people you identified as having the authority to help carry that decision through to its ultimate conclusion must have clear support from the leader. Are you confident that those around them are sufficiently briefed and support the objectives? Are you confident these change agents have the organizational support they need?

4. Avoid introducing failure

In this last segment I encourage you, the leader, to think about some of the seeds of failure that often leaders unknowingly sow. There are a number of these seeds, and leaders need to be aware of them.

For example, when resources are committed in support of a range of decisions, especially decisions of consequence, the leaders tend to become cheerleaders, which is actually a good thing up to a point.

Where cheerleading becomes problematic is when it is accompanied by an implicit message that "failure is not an option." That implicit message often signals that mistakes are unacceptable, and once people up, down, or across the organization receive such a message, the ability to execute can be compromised.

What messages are you sending regarding the important decisions you recently authorized? Is the feedback free of implicit fear? Decisions can and will change. Are the areas of stress being identified?

Chapter 6

Talk About Success

The thing about success is that it is a complex idea, and it is not always obvious. Those of you reading this know that it means different things to different people. You also know that how people see success differs. When the average person thinks about success, they often have a stereotypical view of that word.

When they hear someone talk about success, it is generally in the context of sports figures, a famous author, or someone seen on TV, or in the movies. Let's take this overly broad notion and narrow its focus a little. In the context of a business or other complex organization, leaders and the people who work for them look at success differently.

What thought crosses your mind when you hear the phrase "success builds success"? What about the phrase "success can breed complacency?" Experienced leaders know that both truisms are at work in every business.

They also know that a key task is to find ways to build success, and, at the same time, to mitigate/eliminate the mindset that past successes are proof that you are positioned to continue being successful.

If you have been in the leadership role of an organization for at least five years, the existence of past successes increases the risk of complacency.

Many leaders recognize this as a risk that they must anticipate and mitigate.

In this chapter, I want to look at the relationship between the leader and his/her role in communicating the importance of success to the point it becomes a recognizable aspect of the leader's personality. Much of what I write about has applicability in other walks of life, but the emphasis of this workbook is the modern business leader.

As you look across the business world, there are many successful business leaders. You can find them in old established companies with venerated histories, you can find them in newer companies at the forefront of the latest technologies, and you can find them in areas of business you don't normally think about.

The most successful of these have mastered the art of talking about success in a way that translates into continued success in their companies, and in some instances, increased success that stands out and sometimes becomes iconic. They learned early that talking about success matters, but how you talk about success matters more.

Talking about success is actually telling a story about achieving something out of the ordinary; a story about the building of something around which jobs are created and industries are built.

To older people, the cell phone is a handy way of staying in touch with family, friends and business associates, while other facets of a cell phone can be mysterious and more than a little threatening.

Yet, to the younger generation, the fact that you can make a telephone call is the least of its features.

To them, this is the latest, most mobile platform that gives them the broadest access to a range of social media options.

I was reminded recently of this important fact when it was pointed out to me that Uber, a nine-year-old company, essentially exists as a picture on a cell phone and by touching that picture you can call for the digital version of a taxi. And after only nine years, Uber has a greater market value than 80% of the companies listed on the S&P 500.

It got here because the owners of an "App" went out and told the story of how it works, talked about its success and the customers' satisfaction, and this single App has distorted an entire industry nationally and internationally. Storytelling built around success is a powerful motivator that drives the consumer to venture forth and try something.

When you reach the leadership position that is the focus of this book, you have already experienced one or more painful failures in your careers. You are here now because you avoided the dangerous psychological trap that you are better than others or smarter than others.

Those failures strengthened you so that adversity does not paralyze you, and the passion to persevere still powers your internal engine.

Yet, more importantly, you learned along the way that your success was not due to your efforts alone. You constrained your ego and kept it from getting in your way. When you talk about success, you do it in the context of your company or organization's story.

Along the way, you learned that people in the organization rise or fall based on the quality of your decision-making as a leader, and that status made you accountable to the whole team. That kind of commitment is possible only through passion and perseverance, which is always critical to sustaining a leader's success.

When managers and employees up and down the organization see passion behind the storytelling, it can generate powerful enthusiasm. People will make it *their* story.

It is also through the story that a leader can uproot the seeds of complacency. Ginny Rometti, the CEO and president of IBM, said in one of her speeches that a leader should "never protect the past. If you never protect the past…you will never love it so much that you won't let it go…"

The point she was making is that just because something was successful in the past doesn't mean it will work again, because situations and circumstances always change. Complacency takes root in the belief that if something worked before, then keep doing the thing that worked. It is this mindset that sucks the energy out of all innovation.

Astute leaders learn early to avoid this trap, but it is something that leaders need to consciously look out for, because it can creep into an organization when things are going well and people don't want to rock the boat. It is when things are humming along smoothly that complacency takes root and thrives.

Experienced leaders learn something important about success. It is one of those intangibles that separates leaders from others in the organization.

They learn to define it. At the start of this chapter, I said success is a complex idea and it is not always obvious.

The skillful leader, especially one in charge of a complex organization, learned on his/her way up to that position the importance of being able to first define what success meant for him or her, and then to define it for the larger organization.

And here is what separates the truly great leader from other leaders regardless of how successful they are. When a leader defines success for an organization in a way that allows employees to make it their own, a loyalty to the brand is created within the company.

Employees want to be loyal to the company they work for. They are committing their lives and their futures to that company, so the story has to matter. When I meet with executives, I am sometimes surprised by their readiness to treat employees as a disposable asset and to ignore the consequences of such actions on the future success of the organization.

I point out to them that this behavior unravels the success of the work that goes on around them. When they infect an organization with the perception that an employee is a cog that can be replaced, fear can set in, error rates climb dramatically, and quality suffers. I suspect that you have examples of your own that emphasize this damaging situation.

Two iconic American companies fell into the complacency trap and paid a brutal price. Earlier in this chapter, I used part of a quote by Ginny Rometti of IBM to illustrate what I was saying. The complete quote is as follows: "Never protect the past. If you never protect the past,

"I think you will be willing to never love [it] so much [that] you won't let it go, either. Never define yourself as a product and, in fact, I would augment it; never define yourself by your competition, either.

If you live and define yourself by your product or competition, you will lose sight of who your customer is."

Two companies that failed to understand this rule are Kodak and Xerox. Kodak paid the heaviest price because it was too wedded to the past and failed to innovate at critical points during the past 30 years. It finally fell into bankruptcy in 2012, and as part of its restructuring had to sell most of its patents, worth billions of dollars, at fire sale prices. Kodak came out of bankruptcy in 2013, but its future remains uncertain.

Xerox also waited until it was almost too late. The difference in the two companies was the leader in place at the critical time. In Kodak's case, its leadership wasn't up to the task. In Xerox's case, they had Anne Mulcahy. It is widely recognized that the actions she instigated, led, and implemented across the whole of the organization from 2001 to 2009 are the reasons Xerox remains a Fortune 500 company today and is not just another footnote in the history books.

She quickly recognized that the company was swimming upstream in terms of copiers and services related to copiers. Xerox had waited too long and there were too many competitors offering cheaper, more reliable products, so she took the painful step of abandoning the desktop print device business and laid off the workforce supporting that product line.

It reduced Xerox's workforce by more than 30%. Moreover, she slashed the company's debt by more than 50%, reduced operating expenses by a similar amount, and reduced the non-operational functions to align with her "run lean" objectives.

She then identified the company's critical customers and shifted the company's entire training apparatus to focus on training all remaining employees to support those critical customers. As part of this re-orientation, every employee from senior vice presidents to employees on the loading docks went through the training.

She introduced Six Sigma with stringent benchmarking, alignment, and tracking processes, and she also implemented additional DMAIC processes. All of which was further supported by aggressive cost management. Anything that failed to meet targeted metrics was cut.

What made her efforts ultimately successful was the near total alignment with the requirements of Xerox's critical customers and their needs. Anne Mulcahy mastered the ability to sell each change up and down the Xerox organization. In a 2004 speech, she spoke candidly about how taking the time to talk about the changes, talk about the successes at all levels of the company was fundamental to her success in making the sometimes dramatic changes that were needed.

She stated that many of those successes came at a painful price. Through her efforts, and those of the key people she enlisted, Xerox built on those successes, and they convinced managers and employees at all levels of a now smaller company that there was a future for them.

Sixteen years after she took the helm and eight years since she retired, Xerox still innovates aggressively, still finds ways to succeed, and continues to maintain brand loyalty with its customers.

Twice, in 2005 and 2009, Forbes Magazine recognized Mulcahy as one of America's most influential leaders. Her tenure as a leader is one all leaders should study. One hopes they never find themselves in that particular set of circumstances, but how she achieved success over an extended period of time offers a series of timeless lessons for those in a senior leadership position.

It's Monday morning again and you are once again asked to take this first hour and examine how your methods and practices align with the ideas I explore in this chapter. The first segment this week is intended to direct you to focus on how you communicate success in your leadership role.

As an experienced leader you no doubt understand the importance of talking about success. One of the key questions I want you to explore in this first segment is whether you are as effective in this task as you should be.

In an earlier chapter, I discussed the importance of listening, and why the lack of this skill can harm an organization. The good news here is that even if some CEO's and senior leaders do not communicate well, a good leader can find a trusted lieutenant to assist in telling the success story. History has numerous examples of trusted aides being the leader's voice.

Moses had his brother Aaron, Richard III had John Howard, and General Eisenhower had Omar Bradley. Many other examples give evidence to the fact that, while the success story has to be told, it doesn't always have to be the leader's job.

It is always better if the leader can tell the success story as Anne Mulcahy does, as it makes the message more powerful and relevant, but ultimately the goal is to tell the story.

1.   What did you talk about?

Hindsight, as the sages say, is easy. We can look back and connect the things that worked and the things that did not work, and recognize how it all tied together. What you are asked to do here is to look at those connections and review how you talked about them.

What did you say to the leadership team that supports you? What did you say to your employees over the past week or more about the things that worked and those that didn't?

If you did not speak to them about the important things, will they hear you when it comes to the story you want to tell, the story you want them to make their own? Inherent in these questions is the notion that it is not your successes that baseline the storytelling, it is often other people's contributions to the things that are making your company/organization successful.

This is the *why* that underlies this need to talk about success, because it is the contribution of others to the story that matters, sometimes more than anything else.

During this segment, examine what was spoken about, who said it, who was recognized, and how this was made part of the story.

2.   Think about what really matters

Now that you have identified and have written down what you want to think through regarding the issues you focused on last week, and how they were "messaged," your task in these next few minutes is to examine how that messaging helped or hindered the success story that is your responsibility to keep fresh in the minds of all who work in the company/organization.

Think about the four categories of issues that were identified in Chapter One. In this exercise, examine how you discussed the success you are having or want to have in the context of important issues such as these. Did you focus on details at the right time? Or did the emphasis on details distract from the message and the story you want told?

It is during this segment that you have to determine if you are telling a success story that will ultimately drive the cultural changes that create brand loyalty and the loyalty of your employees. Discussions that drive needs, actions, targets, objectives, and deliverables often take paramount place in the minds of everyone up and down the organization, because that is what the leader talks about.

I do not diminish the importance of these elements in the day-to-day communication that must go on in the everyday life of any organization. But does the success story stand apart and get lost in all the details that people wrestle with, or is the success story part and parcel with the rest?

3. Selling the Story

Telling the story and selling the story are one of those connections that is important to examine to see how well you are doing. Authors Nick Nanton and J.W. Dicks, in a recent article on being the change agent behind building a brand, talked about the importance of story selling as part of the leader's narrative.

At the heart of their discussion is the notion that smaller companies can compete with larger companies if the story is believed, first by those in the company and then by the customer. As the leader, it is just as important to tell the story of small successes as it is to talk about large, important successes.

When leaders tie the smaller stories, which are often more humanizing, to the larger stories, everyone becomes the storyteller. In this segment, you are again asked to look six to eight weeks out and examine the things that your plan(s) indicate are the critical issues coming up during that time frame. Look at the events, changes, and initiatives that are part of your current narrative, and ask yourself during this segment how this narrative might impact those planned tasks.

Whether you are the leader of a company or a large organization, the role you have, demands that you be focused, practical, and data-driven. Some would see these requirements as impediments to the story selling process, but they can actually help. Any good story needs a foundation, what authors would call a plot, and a good leader can use these skills to develop the plot (foundation) for the things large and small that he wants to sell to the employees throughout the company.

So look at the narratives that you recently initiated and expect to carry forward, and examine the foundation underlying the narratives. Will they support or adversely affect the planned events six to eight weeks out? Does what you communicated align with the tasks and actions?

4.   Don't make Assumptions

This subject is one in which it is easy to jump ahead and say to yourself, "I should have done that." It is a natural tendency, but one that should be kept reined in. As I have stated in earlier chapters, the purpose in this last segment is to get the questions right.

Now that you have examined the recent past and looked forward, you have thoughts, conclusions, and questions. This segment is about the questions you have in mind. Begin writing down the questions and rank them in a preliminary way. Think about those you want to personally develop answers to; they should be no more than one or two.

Examine the remaining questions and determine which you want to discuss with your closest advisor, and which you want to have members of your leadership team pursue. The narratives you have ongoing are intended to tell people throughout the organization about what is happening, but are you talking about success?

Chapter 7

Risk: The Modern Day Obstacle

CEOs and senior executives must manage risk. That is the reality of the world in which we all operate. Companies and more than a few large organizations commit significant resources to identifying, quantifying, and managing risk. It is not an exaggeration to state that risk management permeates almost every department of a company's structure.

So much money is spent in this area that no senior manager wants to admit that their efforts are not achieving the results they want. Yet, the reality is often more dismal than they realize. Anyone in a senior position is highly sensitive to the gap between expectations and reality, because the consequence can be severe.

The existence of this gap forces CEOs, board members, and senior managers in high risk positions to carry personal liability insurance. To not do so in today's litigious environment would be outright foolish.

For the purpose of this chapter, the issue of risk falls into two general areas: financial risk and non-financial risk. I will touch briefly on each type, yet the focus here is not the gap referenced above, but more specifically on the behaviors that are a consequence of that gap. Behaviors and consequences that flow from risk-based decisions don't get the attention they deserve.

Managers, supervisors, and employees are quick to take their cues from senior leadership. A clear consequence that comes out of decisions made at the C-suite level is that no one wants to be responsible for risk-management decisions at the operational level. This is particularly true in the non-financial areas of a company's structure.

Because of this general aversion to operational risk, such duties and responsibilities are often assigned to a specific department tasked with overseeing the implementation of principles and standards. Those departments are also charged with assuring that controls are in place and compliance is carried out.

The decision to create a separate department for risk management, or a section within a department, produces consequences. One of the more important consequences is that none of the company's overarching principles, requirements, and standards are embedded in how people think about their work on a day-to-day basis. At best, managers, supervisors, and employees have a limited understanding of what it takes to manage risk and compliance issues.

Furthermore, the departments tasked with principles and compliance oversight rarely have more than a limited understanding of how to manage risk within the business context. Instead, they focus on simply adhering to formal standards and providing evidence that appropriate controls are in place. For example, accountants and financial personnel maintain strong quality controls in all accounting and financial areas to mitigate and/or prevent errors that can have tax consequences.

Those controls work with other controls to assure that errors in the financial arena do not cause any real harm. It requires little effort to link those quality control initiatives to the broader quality assurance objectives of the company and to corporate risk activities. But as we all know, as easy as it is to make those linkages, they not always made, and the consequences are out there for everyone to see.

The same cannot be said on the operational side. At the operations level, departments can and do implement rigorous quality control measures to mitigate or prevent errors that would lead to defects in products or services.

The primary focus of an operational unit is reliability in what is delivered, and there is no connection to the broader risk controls that fall outside a department's immediate objectives.

The linkage of an operational unit's quality control process to the larger quality assurance requirement of a company is based almost entirely on the reliability of the deliverables. Businesses exist to deliver a safe and reliable product or service at reasonable price, and at the same time, they must answer to requirements and standards that are imposed by state and federal authorities.

The challenge to do both creates a level of risk that cannot be completely eliminated. It can be reduced or mitigated, but the fact that risk is always present is at the heart of every decision to make it someone else's responsibility.

A second major consequence of this separation between the compliance functions and day- to-day operations is the cost involved. Companies and organizations must hire people with skills to carry out compliance-based obligations on behalf of the company. These employees reach into all operational units to gather data, analyze systems and processes, and establish linkage between the business units and the overall risk to the company.

The data-gathering and analytical systems to accomplish this are costly. In many companies, the people carrying out compliance-related obligations represent one of the highest contributors to the overall cost of doing business.

Employees outside of senior management view compliance-related matters as someone else's responsibility. They know that a compliance department person will periodically come through and check their work.

They recognize that it is an outside force they will need to react to if a non-compliance situation is found, but in a broader context, it doesn't alter their approach to their work nor their behavior.

Here is where the gap begins to build that I mentioned in the opening paragraphs. If an employee sees no relationship between his or her work and the broader company-based risk, beyond an obligation to fill out a form periodically, the employee will not alter behavior to take that risk into account. It does not become part of the work culture. I will talk more about this in the next chapter.

The common misconception is that the employee is being irresponsible in approaching his or her work, but that is not the case. The truth is that employees have not been trained to recognize the critical connection between the work they do and the broader risk to the company.

Employees are trained to do their work reliably, on time, and safely, so as not to cause personal injury or injury to someone else, but the association to the broader company-based risk is often not part of an employee's regular training. Most leaders know there is a difference between what a leader sees as important and what the average employee sees as important. What is surprising is how many companies fail at bridging that gap.

Here it is appropriate to move from the general to the specific. By exploring circumstances surrounding a particular company, we can look at an explicit set of failures as a frame of reference.

Given the number of companies dotting the landscape that operate under a Consent Decree or Deferred Prosecution Agreement from the Department of Justice, there are more than enough examples. Yet, there is one particular egregious example that fits the purpose of this chapter. I believe the breach of public trust demonstrated by Wells Fargo & Company represents a broad systemic failure that will play out largely behind the scenes.

Some attention has been paid to it in the business pages of newspapers, and on television, but beyond that, the lessons behind the multiple failures inside Wells Fargo will need to be learned inside the business community.

First and foremost is the decision by Wells Fargo to engage in what is apparently fraudulent behavior by "cross selling." This simply means the practice of selling an additional product or service to an existing customer. For those of us in the business world, cross selling is a fairly straightforward process, but it carries some clear rules and obligations. The accepted course of action for cross selling is to demonstrate to the customer that there is real value in the added products or services.

Wells Fargo, in a particularly Orwellian twist, "sold" customers additional products and services, but Well Fargo didn't tell the customers they were receiving anything. They then billed customers for purchases the customer did not know about, assessed fees, and even assessed late penalties. Later, when customers complained, the records were cleaned up. Wells Fargo charged an estimated 3.5 million customers interest and fees on various types of fake accounts, and yet this fraud produced a surprisingly small amount of money.

In this case, employees up and down the chain of command abandoned virtually any adherence to corporate compliance objectives and any commitment to ethics or standards of behavior. What is becoming increasing clear as this sordid tale plays out in various lawsuits is that virtually everyone knew this practice was going on and deliberately hid it from company auditors and bank regulators.

At the time the scandal erupted and became public knowledge in 2015, the current CEO, Mr. John Stumpf, and the current board of directors had known about the unethical practices since 2013. Yet, they did not cancel the program at that point.

Their sales incentive program based on cross selling was allowed to continue until the end of 2014, a period of more than a year and a half. Additionally, senior managers up and down the chain of command knew of the mismanagement of the incentive program and did nothing to correct it for almost six years.

Nothing describes the cultural miasma that permeated Wells Fargo more than its highly publicized launch of a corporate ethics review in 2013. With much fanfare, Wells Fargo issued a series of press releases to explain that it was doing this to better align its compliance and ethical practices with that of the banking industry as a whole.

It was deemed a prudent thing for the bank to do, even though "...the bank prides itself in its strong code of ethics already in place and credits its ethical business practices as being a cornerstone of the bank's culture..." This stunning display of cognitive dissonance is a telling example of the hypocrisy that was so pervasive.

In this week's exercise, you are asked to look at your company or organization and think about the gap this chapter presents. Recognizing, as you surely do, that you work hard to communicate your company's goals and objectives to managers and employees alike, think about recent examples in your own organization where a disconnect occurred between the message and the outcome.

I suspect that, for more than a few reading this book, this subject is familiar, and that you have struggled with this gap before.

1.   Reading the Landscape

During the first segment of this week's exercise, where you think about what happened last week and sift through the events, conversations, instructions, and observations, consider those things in the context of what can be missed in translation from the message to the action.

As you identify four items from the previous week that you want to focus on, what is starting to stand out?
Anyone who has been around for a while knows that company-wide risk must be understood by everyone from the person working the loading dock to the person sitting in the office across from the CEO.

But every CEO/leader knows that isn't the case. Do the actions/initiatives selected this week align with the gap between expectation and reality and work to overcome it? For example, in hospitals, the first line of defense against life-threatening bacteria and viruses is the person who cleans the rooms and halls – the janitor.

For many years quality control and patient safety initiatives had focused everywhere except on the janitors. Only in recent years has common sense reared its head and awakened hospitals to the reality that was in front of them; a critical component, if not completely ignored, certainly was not given the priority it deserved. Company-wide and systems-wide risk is now being incorporated from the "shop floor to the top floor." Other companies are awakening to this necessary mindset, but they still have far to go. What do you see in your organization?

2. Finding the Gap

After you've written down the four issues that stuck out during the first segment, examine these issues from the context of how you incorporated the company-wide risk objectives into the discussions and the decisions. As noted in Chapter I, this scrutiny is not intended to be a review of the mechanics and risk assessment tools your company uses.

This is the point where you ask yourself, "what did I miss?" At the end of this segment you may feel confident that you looked at these issues and that you made reasonable efforts to bridge the gap discussed in this chapter.

McKinsey&Company, in a recent article, reminded its clients and followers that the CEO and other senior leaders understand the controls that are in place to manage risk. Based on the controls in place, the leadership understands "where to accept the risk and where to mitigate for it…"

The reality is that the further from the corner office one goes, the less precise that understanding becomes and the less reliable is the framework for controlling risk. Far too many CEOs and other leaders see the effort required to keep on top of this problem and, rather than shoulder it, they default and transfer responsibility to the compliance group.

The consequence is that when the compliance manager needs to provide information or obtain feedback from the leader, he or she becomes one more demand on the leader's time. The issues to be raised have to be fitted into the schedule, and the CEO/leader never has enough time to truly address the obstacles.

The questions you need to think about as you move into the third segment should be built around the idea that at some point within the distance between your conversations and actions, the framework will weaken. What can you do to anticipate where that weakness might occur? Can you readily identify potential stress points, and is there flexibility to shore up risk management controls the further you go?

Instead of placing responsibility solely on the outside group, compliance, can you find means and opportunity within the department to use the compliance process at key operational points?

3.   Bridging the Gap

My observations in this chapter are by no means unique. Others have noted that companies found to have engaged in truly egregious behavior also have impressive compliance programs and ethics policies and procedures – on paper. Lofty concepts and the rhetoric supporting those concepts are not enough. A structure that is built and then ignored creates fertile ground for risks to propagate.

As you look out six to eight weeks and examine the major features of that landscape in front of you, what do you need to look for, and how, then, do you identify the risks that existing actions and initiatives may be generating? You already know the people responsible for getting you to those mileposts.

Are there conversations, based on the themes discussed here, that you should have with key players?

When you read about the ethical lapses of other leaders, how are these examined? Does your existing compliance program have sufficient depth to scrutinize your company's processes and procedures and test for similar risks?

Do your key managers have conversations about the observed failures in the context of lessons that can be applied in your operations?

4.   Confidence versus overconfidence

The last segment in each chapter contains a recurring theme that demands you examine your role as the leader of the company or organization you run. You are asked to think about the questions you want to ask yourself concerning who you are as a leader, and once again, this is not about second-guessing yourself or second-guessing the decisions you made last week.

What you are asked to do in the last 15 minutes before that door opens and the tide of the day's activities rush in, is to think about key questions on this subject you want to explore in more depth. Some questions you may want to consider on your own, and one or two you may wish to explore with a mentor or that person in the company whom you trust the most.

A recent article by Nicole Sandford stated that "...In the long run, a positive culture of integrity is the foundation for an effective ethics and compliance program, which, when properly embedded into an organization, can create a competitive advantage and serve as a valuable organizational asset."

The point she was making is that you are planting the seeds of a tree, and the tap root of that tree is the ethics that carry the standards and values which, over the long term, will define your company's culture.

It begins with you. Are you setting the right tone?

Chapter 8

The Arc of Integrity

"...How difficult the task to quench the fire and the pride of private ambition, and to sacrifice ourselves and all our hopes and expectations to the public weal! How few have souls capable of so noble an undertaking!" (Abigail Adams)

As I said earlier in this workbook, you are where you are because you worked harder, you worked longer, and you went the extra mile. Stated differently, your ambition and your drive powered your success. Ambition and drive will now determine how well you succeed in this leadership role.

The road to success breeds two kinds of leaders. One kind keeps his/her integrity intact; the other does not.

Shedding pieces of integrity along the way, leaders of the second type reach a desired position tainted by the question of whether or not they can conduct themselves in an ethical manner. One does not have to look hard to find real-life examples of corporate leaders who failed in spectacular fashion where the seeds of their professional destruction were rooted in less than ethical conduct.

Economic stresses that have plagued the American business landscape for the better part of two decades, and the protracted struggle they engendered, led many companies down paths that may have seemed reasonable, but in fact were invitations for wrongdoing. Public companies continue to struggle in this environment to find value that can be returned to the owners – the shareholders.

Pursuit of this goal sometimes leads to acquisitions and mergers, and to improving the bottom line by laying off thousands of employees. It entices corporate leadership to put in place policies that, instead of promoting innovation and growth, function as a shield for self-serving, unethical behavior.

How does this relate to you? Of the two kinds of leaders mentioned, which one are you? Is your integrity intact? Maybe it is a little tattered around the edges and holding a patch or two - that's okay. If it has essentially held together despite recent struggles, then I sincerely hope this section of the workbook will be of value to you.

I phrase it this way because we must deal with a lot of noise in popular culture, and our leaders must be as close to perfect as possible. Yet, even the best of us lead imperfect lives. Successful leaders catch their mistakes and quickly correct them. Good leaders do not allow gaps to form between the error and the action to correct it.

Before going further, we need to a take a few minutes to review the word "morality" and its absence in the business environment.

I want to state up front that this is not about forming judgments or replacing standards of behavior with a set of moral commandments. Leaders do themselves an injustice, however, and make it harder to succeed – especially in large complex organizations – when they don't invest time in considering the moral dimensions of their actions.

If you look at the individuals who make up your organization, you'll find that, with few exceptions, they are law-abiding, responsible people who see themselves as living moral lives.

Whether they are religious or agnostic about matters of faith, they see themselves as knowing the difference between right and wrong.

Morality is the foundation on which such principles such as equity, fairness, ethics, loyalty, and tolerance ultimately rest. Consequently, any efforts to build an ethical culture must begin with a leader whose integrity is clear and unquestioned. He or she lives a moral life. Again, perfection is not the goal, but a visible path must exist showing that decisions were made clearly and openly for the right reason.

In my ethics training seminars, I use a model that helps potential leaders make the right choices, and I do this under the general theme of doing the Right Thing at the Right Time for the Right Reason®. What my training approach teaches, and what I ask you to think about in this chapter, is that doing the right thing is relatively easy to identify if you have a good moral foundation.

Successful leaders separate themselves from issues that can lead them in the wrong direction. You are no doubt sufficiently self-aware to know whether or not you are seen by those around you as a person who has integrity. Let's look at a simple question: do you believe you have the moral authority to convince employees of their value, both as individuals and as employees of the company?

For a company to be seen as ethical, ethics must be a clear and core component of its culture, and for that to be true, a company must have the loyalty of its employees. Unfortunately, many company leaders today believe wrongly that their employees are loyal and committed. Between the level of loyalty in a company and the integrity of its leader exists a clear link. The source of that linkage is the unspoken moral foundation on which the leader builds his or her integrity.

> "...Virtue's true reward is happiness itself, for which the virtuous work, whereas if they worked for honor, it would no longer be virtue, but ambition." (Thomas Aquinas)

It is tempting to read this quote and dismiss our entire discussion of morality, but true leadership contains a strong moral foundation. There was a time in our culture when moral character traits were called virtues, were described as "hard earned," and once earned were guarded.

To protect their "virtuous" image, leaders were careful in their speech and cautious about who they hired or did business with. They would forego potential profit if it put their reputations at risk.

Today's leaders are driven by pressures that create great risk to them personally as well as professionally, and more than a few are willing to take that risk. They believe the payoff justifies the threat, a mindset supported by social science literature. And indeed, the payoff for leaders of many large companies and organizations include a great deal of money, widespread privileges, and extensive power.

The enormity of the payoff creates an isolation that sometimes instills in leaders the mindset that they know more than those around them and can do things others cannot.-They feel it's okay to take risks others would not. Perhaps this is true, but no amount of risk-mitigation processes or procedures will inoculate companies and their leaders if the actions being taken are unethical.

The point I make here is that carelessness of ethics always begins at the top. A leader whose integrity is intact understands that ethical compromises usually start small, and the smallest often have the potential to cause the greatest harm.

Ultimately, it doesn't matter how many other compromises are made, it is that first compromise that starts the decent and the inevitable consequence.

Investigators of accidents resulting in loss of life frequently find that not one but a series of compromises caused the accident. Risk of failure grows with each compromise, and once that first small step is taken, rarely does a path revert back to its original course. The new path is set, and so is the eventual consequence.

The same truth applies to integrity – anyone's integrity. When an individual compromises integrity, the resulting adverse consequences not only impact him or her ~~but~~ often the family as well.

When the leader of a company or an organization compromises integrity, adverse consequences can have far reaching repercussions. Many people suffered a tragic aftermath from the collapse of WorldCom and Enron, and those corporate failures are largely traceable to the unethical actions of the companies' leaders.

What does all this mean to you? The answer speaks directly to how you communicate and conduct yourself personally and professionally. Do you talk about integrity? Do your actions and decisions reflect the values you talk about?

In each chapter, I highlight a specific example to help anchor how you think about the current subject. This week's focus will be a legendary corporate leader who personified what leadership with integrity looks like: former CEO of the General Electric Company, Jack Welch.

It is axiomatic that any serious contender for a leadership role in either a company or an organization should read <u>Jack: Straight from the Gut</u>.

If you have read his memoir you undoubtedly were fascinated, enthralled, shocked, bored and motivated at certain points, but ultimately you must have been impressed by this man's achievements at the reins of General Electric.

When he took over as CEO in 1980, GE had a market value of $1.5 billion, and when he stepped down as Chairman of the Board, GE had a market value of $12 billion.

Jack Welch did not buy companies to improve the bottom line. He in fact, sold any division that was not first or second in its industry, and he laid off one out every four employees. The hard truth Jack recognized was that certain of GE's groups, departments, and functions dated from previous decades, represented obsolete work and were consistently losing money. Jack saw the writing on the wall of this nearly 90-year-old company and shed those operations.

It is important to note that, based on interviews in <u>Jack: Straight from the Gut</u> and works by other writers, Jack Welch communicated his vision unmistakably. He let every employee know what he saw as necessary for the company to succeed long term. He was open and forthright about what he could save and what he could not, and he made no apologies for what must be done. It is also important to note that, for employees who were laid off, he did far more than most companies of that era to ease the impact.

From start to finish, Jack Welch was seen as a man of integrity, because he did not merely talk the talk, he acted on his beliefs. He did not merely emphasize ethics in public, he spoke adamantly about integrity and ethics at just about every meeting he chaired.

As CEO he made the point of stating that integrity was more than just ethics. He was looking for character in his leaders, because he wanted a company that reflected the character of its leaders.

The hour is at hand and once again you are asked to look at the decisions you made last week, to think about actions you took, and to reflect on what you talked about to your leadership team.

At several points in this workbook, I believed it prudent to remind you that this is not about second-guessing the decisions you made or your subsequent instructions and recommendations.

The focus of the first segment, as you sift through the week's events and conversations, is to notice what stands out in your mind and select those items you want to look at more closely.

At the end of the first segment, you will have identified at least four to focus on during this hour. Remember to take a moment before this segment ends to write down your choices.

1.   Who Stands With You?

Now that you have a list for this week, examine the items you chose in the context of the team members who are your strongest allies in making the integrity message an organic part of your leadership.

Leaders often believe they have the wherewithal to stand alone on truly important issues. But in complex organizations that mindset is a trap that weakens a leader's obligation to delegate, especially if he or she does not have a strong supporting team.

The reality is that we are influenced by those around us, and it is important that they are capable and trustworthy. If so, they are your greatest asset in the pursuit of a company deemed by the public to have integrity.

Do you have a strong team? Based upon the items you selected, did you reinforce their confidence in you? Did you convey your confidence in them?

2.   Validate the Values

Does your company have a strong list of values and do they form part of your daily checklist? When you separate issues from the tensions and demands of the day, you can sometimes see gaps that should have been obvious but were not. Gaps can be masked for many reasons.

Looking at things in isolation exposes what was hidden. As you look over the list of issues selected, ask yourself two key questions:

- Were any of the company's values ignored or downplayed in one or more of the actions taken?
- Were any of the actions taken wrapped in window dressing so as to make them more acceptable to people who must carry out the actions?

3. Search for Connections

In this book, I note the fact that a leader's scarcest resource is time. It is a topic found in most books about leadership, and in one form or another each of those books tries to help a leader manage everything he or she does within the constraints that time imposes.

Finding an hour or even a few minutes on an extraordinarily crowded calendar to accommodate one more item is a challenge leaders continually face and only a can appreciate.

Because of this, it is imperative that a leader identifies those moments where personal connection matters most. Such basic human interactions as taking a key team member to lunch or stopping by a break room to spend a few minutes with the employees can create powerful connections.

Those connections are the means by which a leader becomes authentic to the team and connected to their world. Through these simple interactions, a leader establishes credibility. Later, when he or she speaks about integrity, the message is believed.

4. Speak with purpose

Ethics and Integrity are visible character traits in a leader, and equally visible is their absence. Through your words and actions, you demonstrate that you believe Integrity is one of the pillars on which the company or organization stands.

Speak clearly and with purpose about your obligation to help build and lead an organization in which integrity is a "coin of great worth."

To test where you are, notice whether you have asked yourself and your team these two questions:
- Are we staying true to the course?
- Do we understand what we are doing and why?

Any uncertainty in the feedback you receive is a warning sign that should not be ignored.

In this fourth segment of the hour, when you meet with your key advisor, confidant, or mentor, be sure to discuss what's out there that can potentially work against people doing the right thing. Are you guilty of ignoring warning signs from key staff members? Warning signs such as, "This sounds like a great idea, but we don't have any time in the schedule to include it," can easily be disregarded when you aren't focused on listening to them.

Leading by example is a truism that has stood the test of time for a reason. It matters how a leader conducts him- or-herself, and it matters what they say in the context of the actions they take. When leaders act with a clear purpose that reflects who they are and what they stand for, any change required or any message put forth will be more readily believed and accepted.

Getting people to take risks on behalf of the company happens when the leader shows commitment to also taking those risks. And if an answer is needed, state it clearly. Make sure everyone hears it.

Chapter 9

Conflict and the Unresolved Battles

Why think about conflict first thing Monday morning? I placed this issue at the conclusion of this book as I believe this subject is more often than not is looked at by senior leaders after the fact. You are more often than not brought into a conflict issue after things break down.

If you use the analogy of a pothole, you immediately think about a hole in the pavement of one or more streets that you encounter on your way to work. A pothole in the street is a source of irritation because you know it may be awhile before the city or the county gets around to fixing it.

If it irritates you enough, you may even call the public works department and complain, and they may or may not jump on it right away. On the other hand, a pothole in your company parking areas gets an almost immediate response.

It's a safety risk and an eyesore that you do not want to see ignored. Not acting sets a bad example as well as reflecting badly on the company when potential clients visit your location.

Conflict in the workplace occurs every day. You and I know this and the reality is on any given day, in an organization of any meaningful size, a thousand conflicts can occur. Almost all of them are resolved; some easily, some less easily, some quickly, some more slowly, but they get resolved right there where the conflict occurred.

A small percentage do not get resolved.

The literature says that number is somewhere between five and nine percent. These are the potholes, yet unlike the holes in the street or in your parking areas at your company, these cannot be easily seen.

They can be if you know how to look for them. The reality is that supervisors and managers up and down the chain of command are trained to react to visible conflicts after they begin to impact the people involved and the work they do. They are trained to resolve (as opposed to solving) the conflict, or failing that to mitigate the effects of the conflict.

When mitigation fails, the issues escalate with even more adverse consequences that all leaders are well aware of. Most experience leaders understand the problems created when conflict escalates, but I thing a brief aside on this is an important context for this week's exercise.

Once a conflict escalates beyond a certain point, there are only two ways to resolve a dispute. One is through litigation and the second is through the process called alternative dispute resolution which offers a range of options for crafting a solution. The problem with either option is that you no longer have any control over the outcome.

The outcome will be influenced, sometimes significantly, by third parties and when third parties come in to clear things up there can be a different set of consequences that an organization's leadership would prefer not to deal with.

This chapter asks the leader to think about the conflicts he or she is not seeing even among his/her leadership team. It is unreasonable to expect a leader to see the metaphorical pothole three, four, or five levels below him, but his team cannot see them either if he/she does not look for them at his/her level and then ask himself how he missed it?

So what does the leader do differently to help expose the previously unseen pothole? One of the first questions a leader should be asking is what created the pothole? By this I mean what were the repetitive pressures that wore at and weakened the structure?

By now you, the leader, used the process outlined in this book on several occasions, and it is my expectation that you derived some level of benefit, and when you continue to use this process in the future, the benefits will be clearer. This chapter asks leaders to focus on what is not easily seen, but before moving through this chapter, a type of conflict exists that can be seen, yet it is often ignored.

These are the potential conflicts that loom large, and you can see them, but they are future potential conflicts. This chapter would not be complete if we did not take a moment to talk about certain conflicts that represent the proverbial elephant in the room.

Every experience leader knows that he/she will contend with a group of issues that affect the character and nature of the company or organization they lead. The need to address these issues is itself a potential source of conflict, which is why many executives tread lightly. These potential conflicts require that leaders put in place plans to resolve the problem(s) before they become problems.

One example of a potential conflict occurs around who will succeed the current owner, CEO, or partner. In many companies this plan is already in place and it undergoes a periodic review to make sure it's still aligned with the requirements of the organization's board and other key stakeholders.

However, in some companies a strong negative inertia exists that prevents this requirements from being fulfilled in a timely manner. Many examples exist of companies that go through the tumult of a change in leadership because they failed to properly plan for this eventuality.

It is rare for companies to repeat this process because, having gone through this tumult once, they will make doubly sure they don't experience that level of disruption again. But some companies don't learn, and one that comes to mind is The Walt Disney Company.

Walt Disney ran his company under a tight hierarchy that he controlled, and while there were periodic discussions about who would run the company after he retired, those discussions were never formalized to the point a true succession plan could be implemented. Walt Disney died in 1966 after a short battle with cancer, and it left the company without a clear leader.

Over the next 20 years a number of CEO were brought on board by Roy Disney, Walt's nephew, and these leaders reported to Roy Disney and his close ally on the board, Sid Bass. Because of the company's vulnerability, their primary goal was to stay independent and not be taken over by other companies. As a result, the company failed to invest in new talent, failed to innovate, and was falling further behind in an industry it once dominated.

They finally realized they needed to turn the company over to someone who could lead the company through the major changes needed to position the company for badly needed growth. Roy Disney and his allies on the board brought in Michael Eisner to take the helm. He was far more successful than they envisioned.

Yet, the relationship between Roy Disney and Michael Eisner was neve smooth or easy because Roy continued to intrude into the management decisions that were Eisner's responsibility.

Because of Roy Disney's influence, the board once again failed to develop a true succession plan that was not subject to one man's will, nor did they periodically examine, in any true sense of the word, the alternatives if the CEO or members of his immediate leadership team could not continue.

The conflicts between Michael Eisner and Jeffrey Katzenberg and the death of Frank Wells in a helicopter crash exemplify this lack of a formalize process. All of which was greatly exacerbated by the poorly thought out decision to hire Michael Ovitz, which ultimately cost the company an estimated $150 million dollars and resulted in a lawsuit that lasted almost ten years.

The last few years of Eisner's time at the helm of Disney was defined by his tense relationship with the board of directors. The hostility between the board and Eisner forced him to resign more than a year ahead of schedule after selecting Bob Iger as his successor.

Today Mr. Iger is about to continue his role as CEO of the Walt Disney Company; having agreed to a third extension of his contract because the company has not found a suitable replacement.

The Walt Disney Company achieved great success in the past 30 years, but that success is tempered by the some hard truths that merit a far more detailed examination.

I believe a linkage exists between large problems that go unsolved and smaller problems that are often unseen and also go unresolved.

In the first segment for this week, and as you focus on the issues of the past week that stand out; think in terms of conflict and controversy. Think about those things that stand out not because of the pressing problems they represented, but look at them and think about the underlying conflict or controversy.

1. The Disagreement

Disagreements exist that are obvious. Because dealing with disagreements create uncertainty and leave people feeling unsure how to proceed, these disagreements are frequently re-defined as problems. Bingo! A problem is solvable.

Leaders, executives, managers, and supervisors are trained to deal with problems, so change a dispute into a problem and everyone starts thinking about solutions and no one has to think about the disagreement any more. Sound familiar?

Just as conflict is a fact of life, disagreements are also a fact of life. The challenge is recognizing that disagreements drive conflict. Up and down the organization, disagreements occur every day because see their tasks differently. For example, a team is assembled to tackle a project or a piece of a project.

The members of that team will see and speak about a solution or set of solutions and not everyone will agree because their approach is different from someone else's proposed method.

Some on the team have stronger personalities and other members of the team may coalesce around that person, but not everyone. There will be one or two holdouts who will insist that their approach be given equal consideration.

Here is the key disagreement – the true lack of consensus. How, as the CEO or as member of the leadership team do you address a lack of consensus? In the decisions you made or participated in last week, did you take time to expose that lack of consensus? Did you bring it out in the open and discuss it? Do you know how wide or deep it is?

2. Unwrapping the Disagreement

If you do not solve the disagreement, somewhere down the line a conflict will force you to act, and you will be at a disadvantage all the way through that resolution process.

So how does one proceed? My work as a mediator showed me very early what all mediators quickly learn and that is a conflict typically has many layers, and successful mediators help the parties in a dispute unwrap those layers.

Getting to the heart of a disagreement is very much like a mediation in that you have to go through this unwrapping process, and let's be candid, many leaders know this. You and other leaders may not talk about it in this way, but you recognize that in a disagreement you have to figure out what's driving the individuals involved, and this takes time. You cannot build a consensus without going through this process first.

Most leaders, whether in a senior position in a company or, further down the chain quickly become frustrated by the amount of time it takes to build consensus. Managers and supervisors are especially sensitive to the amount of time it takes to build consensus because they work closest to those executing the work, and feel the heat and pressure to get things done on schedule.

They are the one in the chain most likely to seek work arounds to get "it" done on time and pretty much ignoring the pothole until the proverbial axle breaks, a cloud of dust flies up, and everything goes south.

In this second quarter hour the goal is to think about the steps that you took with regard to those issues you have mentally highlighted. This segment asks you to think about how you worked those issues that contained conflict and controversy.

Let's start with a question leaders often avoid asking – did I cut things short and move to a decision too quickly? It is not a question to drive introspection. It is a gut check question that you need to ask yourself, and you will know in retrospect whether or not you gave the issues enough time.

Each company and organization is different, and it is important that, as the leader, you develop a set of questions that helps you review the previous week's issues.

3. Seeing yet Not Seeing

In the third quarter hour, I ask the reader to look six to eight weeks in to the future. This chapter is about seeing what those around you are too busy to see. Your company/organization has employees tasked with managing discrete pieces of work, and you have systems in place designed to aid those responsible for those tasks.

These graphs, charts, and schedules tie multiple strings of activities together. You and your leadership team have processes and procedures in place to guide your examination of these multiple tasks and how they relate to each other.

You are accustomed to looking at those areas for potential delays and potential conflicts. However, the conflicts you look for are not conflicts within the meaning of this chapter. The conflicts you traditionally address are actually symptoms of schedule problems.

Among the many duties a project manager has, one of the most important tasks is to anticipate problems and work to resolve them before they become actual scheduling problems. As tempting as it is to continue to look at near future activities within this context, the goal of this section of the exercise is ask you, as the leader, to look at those potential areas of conflict that may occur that others don't normally look at because they don't see that larger picture.

Who are the key players within your organization? Who are the key players among the other stakeholder – the customer, the supplier, the shipping company? It is one thing to look at where the flow of work may be constrained six to eight weeks out, but have you looked at the plan/strategy for dealing with the constraints from the standpoint of the disagreements this will create?

Or are you focusing on the mechanics around overcoming the constraints should they arise?

4.   The Conflict Triangle

In the introduction to this book I cautioned that you would not find a lot of charts, graphs, or images. I explained that the image of a ticking clock would appear a number of times to emphasize that what you are doing is creating a discipline with a defined time period.

In concluding this book, I want to the leader to focus on the idea that any structure requires actions and/or designs that add strength to the structure. A building's strength does not come from the size of its beams, but how angles such as triangles are used to reinforce the basic shape of the building.

As experienced leaders many of you are experienced in resolving conflict. This chapter asked you to take a deeper look at how you apply those skills.

The three corners of this triangle are:

1. Separation – Your experience taught you that you have to stop people from arguing with each other over who is right or who is wrong; over who is at fault.

When any disagreement escalates into conflict, people build defensive positions and fortify them with arguments and excuses, and they feel threatened when asked to step back.

Your leadership role over time taught you how to get people to step back from these entrenched positions, or if, the demands of your work prevented you from doing it, you found someone with that skill to separate the people and their emotions from the issues so that the issues could be viewed dispassionately.

In looking forward how can you anticipate this necessary step so that it can be implemented sooner?

2. Basis – The nomenclature or the vocabulary varies from company to company, but the idea is similar across its multiple descriptions, and that is the point the leader establishes from which the parties can explore alternatives.

That point is the metaphorical distance between the parties and issues such that constructive discussions of alternatives can proceed without the parties feeling they have to retreat behind their previous defensive position.

Looking outward six to eight weeks in the context of identifying a basis (that metaphorical starting point) for defusing conflict is a challenge to accomplish in a fifteen minute segment.

Yet, it is an inherent part of this exercise to look at anticipating how disputes can aggravate the inevitable schedule constraints that arise in any work environment. Since every workplace has unique characteristics, how would you take advantage of those unique aspects of your business to assist you in this process?

3. Action – AHA! I can already see you grimace and hunch your shoulders. Every consultant under the sun tells his/her clients about the need for action.

Most will tell their clients such things as prepare a written plan – as if you haven't done that in the past. They will tell you to create a way to measure results – also as if you have never before heard the phrase Key Performance Indicator. Too often you hear stuff you already know; even though we may phrase it differently.

From the standpoint of this chapter and the approach it suggests for handling conflict in the future, there are two things that leaders, even experienced leaders, don't do well.

On matters related to conflict you identify the decision maker early – the sooner the better. That person must be seen as carrying authority over that matter that comes from you and that he/she does not have keep checking with the boss.

Nothing robs a negotiator of his/her credibility faster than the perception that the person doing the talking doesn't have the power to decide. A key question here is have you set your negotiators up for just such a credibility problem?

The second thing often left hanging after the dust settles is ownership. As the leader, you must accept the outcome and make clear that ownership by you is without conditions, and the obligation by the other parties is equally clear and unambiguous.

It is no longer surprising to me how many "deals" become unraveled after the fact because the parties start taking exceptions to what everyone believed was a done deal. Whatever is written must be clear in both its intent and its execution, and that intent and execution needs to be publicly reinforced by you and others on your leadership team.

A key question to ask yourself is, how are you making sure this is happening as it should?

Each chapter in this book asked you to look at the issues described in the context of questions, actions, and possible consequences. By doing this at a set time for set amount of time, the objective was to help create a discipline of thought that will lead to a better discipline of action, and a betterment of your leadership.

I thank you for taking the time to read the book, and it is my sincere wish that you found it helpful.

ABOUT THE AUTHOR

Jerry Cooper is the founder, CEO, and Managing Partner of Cooper Druesne and Cooper (CDC Integrated Services, LLC). This book is the product of almost 40 years as a business owner, manager, consultant, negotiator, mediator, and trainer. He brought to this book a range of unique experiences that formed the foundation for the work he undertook.

Jerry was born in the mountains of eastern Arizona, when that area was one of the major Copper producing areas of country. Of English and Scottish descent, He is the son of a 10th generation miner and can trace his family back to 17th century England and much earlier. While born in Arizona, he and his brothers and sister grew up in Mexico in small mining towns along the spine of Mexico's Sierra Madre Mountains because of his father's work.

As a boy growing up in Mexico, he came in contact with farmers, ranchers, Indians such as the Yaqui and the Tarahumara and learned to hunt and fish from a young age. He learned about his family's history and migration to America before the Revolutionary War, and their westward migration to the iron ore and copper mining areas in the Michigan Upper Peninsula in the early 1840's.

He grew up in areas with few roads, even fewer cars. The absence of television allowed him to grow up listening to radio. When he wasn't listening to a ballgame, he enjoyed the many books his parents had collected.

His father James, a survivor of German POW camps, witnessed much death and destruction, and gave his son one piece of advice…"choose work where things get built. Don't chase money, build your own path, but always work toward making things better".

He chose to work in what we now call the Energy sector with a near constant focus on the building of things. Beginning with a power plant in his home state of Arizona then a pipeline in Alaska, and on to nuclear power plants in California and Washington, then pipelines and platforms in Mexico and Venezuela, and refinery expansions in Texas.

He took what he learned and started his own company and from all of these experiences came the core ideas that are framed within the covers of this book. He is currently working on his second book due out in the fall of 2018.

He and his wife Corinne, their three grown children and two grandsons all make their home in Houston, Texas.